C O O L
W A T E R

COOL
~~~~~~~~~~~~
WATER

*Alcoholism,
Mindfulness,
and Ordinary
Recovery* ~~~~

William Alexander

Calligraphy by Kazuaki Tanahashi

SHAMBHALA
BOSTON & LONDON
1997

Shambhala Publications, Inc.
Horticultural Hall
300 Massachusetts Avenue
Boston, Massachusetts 02115
www.shambhala.com

12 11 10 9 8 7 6

Printed in the United States of America
♾ This edition is printed on acid-free paper that meets the American National Standards Institute Z39.48 Standard.

♻ Shambhala Publications makes every effort to print on recycled paper. For more information please visit us at www.shambhala.com.

Distributed in the United States by Random House, Inc., and in Canada by Random House of Canada Ltd

Library of Congress Cataloging-in-Publication Data

Alexander, William.
    Cool water: alcoholism, mindfulness, and ordinary recovery/
William Alexander.
        p. cm.
    ISBN 978-1-57062-254-0 (pbk.: alk. paper)
        1. Substance abuse—Treatment.   2. Meditation—Therapeutic use.
3. Recovering addicts.   I. Title.
RC564.29.A43   1997   97-11891
362.292′8—dc21   CIP

This book is for Pauline Cerf Alexander
What a marvel that we were born in the same era!

CONTENTS

~~~~~~~~~~~~~~~~~~~~

CONTENTS

ACKNOWLEDGMENTS

AS I HAVE MOVED FROM ISOLATION to connection, I have had the good fortune to meet some very special individuals and to fall in with some powerful communities.

I want to offer my endless gratitude to my formal teacher John Daido Loori at Zen Mountain Monastery (ZMM) at Mt. Tremper, New York. Thank you also to Bonnie Myotai Treace, the first dharma heir to Daido, and Geoffrey Shugen Arnold, who at this writing has received priestly transmission from him. I know that their practice and mine has been supported by both the monastic and lay practitioners at ZMM, so I bow to all members of the Mountain and Rivers Order.

I first met Zen monk Thich Nhat Hanh in the fall of 1992. I was immediately taken with this humble and powerful man. He will no doubt shake his head when he reads this description, but he is, simply, the most spirited and most heartful person I have ever known. He is totally congruent. There is no difference between who he is and how he lives. I feel fortunate to have been with him, in spirit and fact, for the past six years. I am grateful as well to all fellow members of the Community of Mindfulness, the Tiep Hien Order, which he founded. Thanks especially to dharma teachers and dear friends Lyn Fine in New York and Joan Halifax in New Mexico. A special bow to my special friend Tinh Thũy in Plum Village, France.

For their support and encouragement through the process of writing this book and longer, I offer thanks to old friend Sam Keen and my friends Lenny Holzer, Mark Gero, Hugh O'Haire, my agent and special friend Leslie Breed, my dharma sister Mollie Dairyo Brodsky, and my cohort Elene Loecher at the Hazelden Renewal Center. Thanks as well to my new friend David O'Neal at Shambhala Publications.

Without the presence of the worldwide community of Alcoholics Anonymous, this book could never have been written. My love and gratitude to all those courageous people.

Here, finally, are two people without whom . . .

In the spring of 1986 I wandered, by delicious accident, into the Cathedral of St. John the Divine on Manhattan's upper west side. Recklessly, I said I needed to talk to a priest. That reckless accident led me into the thrall, comfort, and finally deep friendship of the Very Reverend James Parks Morton, then the Dean of the Cathedral. Jim spread a safety net for me, and I have yet to find the edges. Thank you Jim, especially for the tears we shed while holding each other, on Good Friday, 1987, as we realized together the deep commonality of the suffering of the human community and the hope of resurrection.

And then there is Emily! I offer this work to my longtime and long lost friend Emily Sell, an editor of extraordinary gifts, who resurfaced at just the right moment to bring this book home in style. Emily, you have enriched my life with your kindness and skill, and I thank you.

Do not pursue the past.
Do not lose yourself in the future.
The past no longer is.
The future has not yet come.
Looking deeply at life as it is
in the very here and now,
the practitioner dwells
in stability and freedom.
We must be diligent today.
To wait till tomorrow is too late.
Death comes unexpectedly.
How can we bargain with it?
The sage calls a person who knows
how to dwell in mindfulness
night and day
'the one who knows
the better way to live alone.'

—from "The Sutra on Knowing the Better Way to Live Alone,"
Bhadderkaratta Sutta (Majjhima Nikaya 131)

Introduction

~~~~~~~~~~~~~~~~~~~~~~~~~~~~~~~~~~~~~~

SOMETHING'S HAPPENING HERE

THE HAZELDEN FOUNDATION is an alcoholism rehabilitation center located on over five hundred roll-
ing acres of trees and grasses just outside the tiny
town of Center City, Minnesota, an hour and a half from the
Minneapolis/St. Paul Municipal Airport. To a casual visitor it
might look like the campus of a well-endowed junior college.
To the anonymous suffering souls who arrive there in the cars
and vans that pick them up from the airport, and who are still
in the ethanol haze from that final final drink before committing to the unknowable life without booze and drugs, it looks
like something else entirely. Visions of heaven, purgatory, and
hell gleam from the polished windows and stone walls.

Hazelden is a place thoroughly informed by Western religious belief and practice. The folks who run it would never say
that and no graduate will defend or attack that statement, but it
is such a place just the same. In a thirty-day stay there, the
drying-out drunk learns about God as we understand *him* (emphasis added), a Higher Power who can relieve the years of
accrued shame of active alcoholism. This is the home of what is
called the Minnesota Model for recovery from alcoholism, and

the program here is solidly planted in the fecund soil of Alcoholics Anonymous (AA). It works; and folks who have stayed sober in AA for years, with or without a Hazelden medallion in their pocket, will tell you that "if it works, don't fix it!"

How could we have explained to that casual visitor, if she had happened to show up on 4 February 1997, exactly what is going on in the Renewal Center at Hazelden, a boomerang-shaped building just around a gentle curve from "Primary," the mother ship of all recovery units? How to explain the smell of temple incense, the ringing of Japanese bells, and the startling sight of a line of seventeen men and women walking ever so slowly, eyes cast down and hands folded in a distinctly unprayerful knot just below their navels, through corridors lined with pictures of AA founder Bill Wilson and display cases of AA memorabilia? And how do you explain it when these same people enter a small room and fold themselves into an awkward position resembling, in some cases more closely than in others, the Lotus position and then how to understand, in this Judeo/Christian enclave, the silent and motionless twenty-five minutes of meditation that follow? No one moves. There is no sound. The incense smoke drifts lazily from a black plastic bowl full of uncooked brown rice. There is an ersatz altar, a coffee table really, decorated only with a pine bough. All this is overseen by a middle-aged man with short graying hair and a bit of a gut peeking out from a curious black bib that is worn over a plaid sports shirt and apparently held together by a circle of polished wood above the left breast. What is going on?

I have just described a moment or two from the first ever Ordinary Recovery retreat at the Hazelden Renewal Center, a six-year-old facility devoted to the support of recovering alcoholics in their day-at-a-time quest for life-long sobriety. It was the first time in the short history of the so-called recovery movement that a bunch of drunks, or other folks whose lives had been seriously affected by alcoholism, joined in the rigorous discipline of seated Zen meditation (zazen), with pure, clear, and shared intention, in an atmosphere of faith, doubt, and effort to get better together. These folks—Henry from Tampa, Ann from Madison, Ottie and Lida from Tucson, and others—jumped into an event never before experienced in such an atmosphere.

I was the guy wearing the little black bib and, with these pioneers, had set out to see what could be done to experience our individual lives and selves in new and exciting ways. The vision of Ordinary Recovery is my own, and these pioneers came to add their eyes to mine.

It worked. By Sunday we had come together, the seventeen of us, in ways we could not have imagined on the previous Tuesday night when we gathered for the first time. Sunday noon, I announced that we would end this retreat with just one more chant. I stood with Elene Loecher, the spiritual director of Renewal Center, and Mollie Brodsky, a Buddhist drunk and good friend who worked with me that week. We stood solemnly for a moment, and when we burst into Roy Rogers' theme "Happy Trails To You," the place came unglued. It got downright inappropriate in that room. Ann from Madison started making a sound somewhere between a laugh and a howl. Ottie and Mary and Kate started to giggle. Bridget beamed. Elene cried tears of gratitude at having heard, just before Roy's song, the wonderful words of T. S. Eliot, ". . . and all shall be well / and all manner of things shall be well."

I vow never to forget those wonderful, gutsy people. We were disciplined in the midst of permissiveness and bold in the face of ghosts and demons. One of us climbed a hill late one afternoon and screamed at God, over and over, "Why?" and then got her answer in the still quiet of early morning zazen.

This was the first experiment with the intensive side of the practice of Ordinary Recovery. It won't be the last. There is a gentler practice as well, one that is simply a matter of connecting with the stuff of the ordinary world and being transformed by it. I realized early on that recovery from alcoholism is rather ordinary and that the real danger is to see it some other way. I saw that I was not special because I was an alcoholic and that to be a *recovering* alcoholic did not make me special either.

That is what Ordinary Recovery is. Not complicated; not special. Any addict, like so many of his brothers and sisters in the larger world, lives a life of rapture and illusion. Ordinary Recovery is about waking up to what is real. When you see what is right before your eyes, you are healed. The way to the healing moment is through paying attention: Pay attention; the medicine is right before you all the time. You are enlightened by the entire phenomenal universe, and "the price is not less than everything."

The world heals you. As the world heals you, you heal the world.

I invite you into this world. I want you to imagine that it is just you and me on this journey. If you'll come along, I'll keep my attention on only you. The pages to follow and the words you're reading right now are yours and mine to share. See how they fit.

Breakdown, Ordinary Recovery, and Autumn Prayers

~~~~~~

All religion begins with the cry "Help."

WILLIAM JAMES

Breakdown, Winter 1996

THE WINDS HURL GROUND FOG and snowmist around the deep snow-covered yard outside my window. The last few days have seen heavy snow, twenty-eight inches here in northern New Jersey. Today the wind and fog and loose snow create a landscape I am accustomed to seeing in paintings by Patricia Reynolds or in old Zen ink drawings of shrouded mountain passes. There is little color; just some orange-browns and steelish greens in the greys and whites and speckled blacks. The finches and chickadees are not coming to the feeder just outside my window. Perhaps the wind is too great. Everything moves.

Thirteen winters ago I lived not so far from here, just across the Hudson River in Manhattan. I had a dreary little room with sparse and uncomfortable furniture at the Chelsea Hotel on Twenty-third Street and Seventh Avenue. That's the place where poets have lived and died, where artists pay their rent with paintings, and where parts of an insufferable movie,

Chelsea Girls, were filmed. There was no glamour in the cluttered lobby that winter. I couldn't fool myself any longer. Romanticism had crumbled, so I drank endlessly and without hope. I was at the end of the road and the Chelsea was the last stop.

As such stories go, the stories of awakening and returning home, this one is on the undramatic side. Your story is different and so are all the stories of all those we love and care for whose lives are diminished or, in the worst cases, snuffed out by the sheer meanness of addiction. But there are similarities in our stories. You may have ended up in the Ritz or a mission, but the devastation is the same. In my story, there are no moments of great redemption, no visitations by angels, at least not of the noncorporeal variety, and no blinding white lights in drunk tanks or hospital rooms. I didn't hear voices and there were no anomalous coincidences to force my hand. I am not a fictional creature and the devices of dramatic fiction don't fit here real well. As undramatic a story as I have to tell, it has all the drama I'll ever need. It was like this: One day I was drunk all day and most of the night; the next day I was sober—and destined to stay that way until this moment at least. If I look deeply enough at this circumstance, it is no surprise. The spirits did, in fact, hang close by my side, waiting their cue. That winter at the Chelsea Hotel I had gone to the ground. The darkness was unavoidable at last, and the dark side wouldn't let me be. If this is familiar to you then we are kin. And I believe that what happened to me and you and all of us who leave our own special Chelseas lies within the inner circle of miracles.

I have now come to see my alcoholism as my dark twin—close dwelling, co-arising at every moment, conceived with me, born with me, and with me still. It is as much a part of me as my eye color, my heart, my spleen and lungs, my choleric temperament, and my gentle hands. For each of us, our dark twin populates a universal landscape of forgetfulness and delusion. We are trapped in a deadly rapture.

Ordinary Recovery

After a few years of recovery, I returned to my longtime affection for the teachings of Zen Buddhism. Over time I began to see how beautifully those teachings dovetailed with the practice of the Twelve Steps of Alcoholics Anonymous. For me, Zen practice amplified and extended what I had begun to find in AA. I saw that recovery from addiction was a gift and that the gift was revealed to me in the ordinary stuff of daily life. So ordinary, this extraordinary gift.

Alcoholism is what I have, so that will be at the core of the stories I will be telling here. This is a book of stories and suggestions that I believe most people can relate to. In AA, we talk of experience, strength, and hope. We use living words.

Please don't hesitate to see your own addiction here. I have written this book for alcoholics and addicts. It is a book about alcoholism—specifically mine. It is not, I emphasize, a book about Zen. I make my living as a teacher and a writer, but in my Zen practice I am a student, not a teacher. I teach Ordinary Recovery, not Zen. What I offer here from that magnificent spiritual tradition is my experience of it. I am a beginner in Zen and in AA and hope I always will be. Shunryu Suzuki said, "In the beginner's mind there are many possibilities, but in the expert's there are few." From beginner to beginner, here are my experience, strength, and hope.

The practice of *mindfulness* is the heart of Ordinary Recovery. Thich Naht Hanh, a Vietnamese Zen Buddhist monk, says that mindfulness is "keeping one's consciousness alive to the present reality." To paraphrase a Zen chestnut, "When hungry, be hungry. When eating, eat." To be mindful is to be fully in the present moment. But driven by a thousand addictions, pushed and pulled by a multitude of distractions, we poor moderns, while "hard-wired for the Paleolithic," in Wes Jackson's felicitous phrase, have little appreciation for the grace of the present moment. We are torn apart, you and I, by the oppressive demands of a national and world culture of increasing materialism, consumerism, and continued violence. A sane person could not watch the evening news without sobbing.

The wider world is often not sane, and living sanely, defined as "wholeminded" in AA, is often not rewarded. For many people, therefore, a practice of mindfulness is the path of wholeness in the midst of chaos. Mindfulness is *not* about relieving stress; it is about putting the sources of stress in perspective. It is a challenging practice, challenging to our assumptions about the world and about ourselves. Mindfulness, then, is the tool of Ordinary Recovery; it is one way to engage the reality of recovery from alcoholism in the midst of cultural chaos.

Our deadening materialistic culture makes outrageous demands on the most mature among us, and the newly recovered alcoholic, deprived of the one beloved coping mechanism and asked to live a *spiritual* life, is singularly raw and bewildered. As an active alcoholic or addict, you lived in a state of chronic apartness, separated from the gods, from the people who loved you, and from your life in the moment by shame, fear, and myriad other emotional toxins. In early recovery you are haunted by the same devils. Although you are counseled to "stay in the now" and "let it go" or "turn it over," there is a scarcity of practical advice on how to do so in a world that seems mad. I recall so many times in my early recovery having some well meaning old-timer tell me, "You're right where you should be. Just keep coming back and it'll get better." Silently I would respond, "Maybe for you, asshole."

A friend who is a treatment professional opined that "booze fighting" is not the greatest threat for recovering people; it is simply staying centered that poses the true threat to sobriety. Alcoholics Anonymous co-founder Bill Wilson believed the future of AA would lie in "maintaining *emotional* sobriety." Booze is never the problem. If you have had problems with alcohol or other drugs, you understand that for years the drugs were the *solution*. I recall driving around Sacramento in the early 1970s with a bunch of friends. We were fresh from a multi-martini lunch with a case of beer in the back seat, carrying a skin full of amphetamines, when we spotted a huge billboard that asked, "Do you have trouble coping with alcohol?" We roared with laughter and my friend Heidi answered the question for us all. "Hell no." She said, "It's coping *without* alcohol that's the problem." It's amazing, isn't it, how the ads that are supposed to help are, to this day, objects of derision? A psychiatrist once said to me, "Don't talk down to an addict. It will only piss them off."

When the booze is gone the problems start and right here, today, the problems are amplified by the sheer rush of the times. We alcoholics lose, in an instant, our familiar old buffer when we put aside alcohol. Instant oblivion is gone. Gone, but always close at hand.

In an often-quoted remark, the Zen teacher Shunryu Suzuki said that the fruits of Buddhist practice are "nothing special." It is not always noted that he also said that the results were "a wondrous power," making the critical distinction that "before you achieve them, they are wondrous. After you achieve them they are nothing special." The idea of sobriety seems wondrous and out of reach to an active drunk for whom the misery of alcoholism is, in fact, homeostasis, the total and only reality. Body, mind, and spirit are in a precarious balance. Ethanol and the liver are engaged in a lethal minuet, and the only remaining certainty in an increasingly ammonia-clouded mind is "I must drink or die."

Gregory Bateson, an anthropologist, cyberneticist, and author of the double bind theory of schizophrenia, says that to a drinking alcoholic, drunkenness is sanity. Conversely, recovery for a sober alcoholic is, or should be, *unexceptional*, while his days of drinking are quite properly viewed as insane. Recovery is ordinary. What is recovered is the ordinary world we left behind. What we realize, drug free, is the transcendent wonder of the very ordinary. What is recovered is teacups and lawn furniture and the crackle of leaves underfoot. We see with an unaccustomed clarity. Dwelling wholly in the ordinary, we are able to know intimately the wonder of God.

The ordinary is sacred. The sacred is ordinary.

The second of the Twelve Steps to recovery in AA is one's coming "to believe that a power greater than ourselves could restore us to sanity." Less remarked upon is the line, "By this time [after completion of steps one through nine] *sanity will have returned* [emphasis added]." What has happened is "a spiritual awakening" (AA, by way of William James), "enlightenment" (in Buddhist terms), "huge emotional displacements and rearrangements" (Carl Jung, in a letter to Bill Wilson), or "simply . . . a change in epistemology." (Gregory Bateson).

Jessamyn West says, "A religious awakening which does not awaken the sleeper to love has roused him in vain." The recovered alcoholic has re-engaged with her human capacity to love and to love actively. Compassion is born from the ashes of isolation. In the pages that follow, we will look at the realization of compassion in the recovered life. As you walk this path of Ordinary Recovery, you need only look beneath your feet if you think you've lost the way. What you are doing right now, with your entire heart and mind, is your recovery. Pay attention! The entire universe is conspiring with you. To succeed you merely have to show up.

Autumn Prayers

Let me offer you two autumn fragments from a larger story, many seasons long.

The first fragment is from the fall of 1994. I had just begun working with the idea of using Buddhist principles in dealing with the dilemmas of long-term freedom from addiction, this process I now call Ordinary Recovery. I wanted to check it out with people whose understanding of both the problem and the solution was greater than mine. To that end, I visited with Don Hewlett, the program director of Fellowship House in New York. Fellowship House is a rehabilitation and ongoing care center established in 1993 by the Hazelden Institute. Don, a former Franciscan monk, is a man of remarkable energy and compassion. We talked at length—weaving theory, story, and opinion—about the pitfalls faced by recov-

ering addicts and alcoholics in the haste and jangles as this
bloody century hobbles to an end. Although Don and I are
from very different backgrounds, we are both active in spiritual practices that include an emphasis on silence and periodic
retreat. And as our talk and storytelling that day went on and
afternoon shadows lengthened, we discovered a deeper shared
understanding of grave obstacles to simply trying to live an
ordinary life in such difficult times and circumstances. We
agreed that, although our concern was for addicts and alcoholics, it's an ordeal for anyone just to have some sense of connection and heartfulness in such mean times. It was somber
talk. Not long before I had to leave to catch a train, and after
a silence that had stretched comfortably for several minutes,
Don said, "You know, what we all need is an altar on every
street corner."

The second fragment is from the fall of 1995. At the Cathedral of St. John the Divine in New York, there is a small
chapel with a striking and mysterious Earth Altar. When I first
saw this altar, on the day of the Feast of St. Francis that year,
I could not approach it. The larger cathedral was filled with
several thousand people, many of whom had brought animals—dogs, cats, screeching parrots, mice, snakes, and gerbils.
Just outside the great bronze doors of the cathedral were a
full-grown male elephant, two llamas, a goat, monkeys, and
myriad other creatures awaiting their dramatic procession to
the high altar. My own over-stimulated "monkey mind" chat-
tered in fractious harmony with my animal mates. I stood
outside the little chapel, hidden away behind the high altar
and breathed deeply, centering and quieting my mind. I entered it, away from the high energy of the great cathedral,
with a mind of awe and wonder. As I approached the altar, I

recalled Zen monks approaching their altars, robes whispering, bare feet slipping on polished floors as incense swirled, while the dharma hall became preternaturally quiet and attention was focused on the figures of Buddhas and Boddhisattvas, seated eternally, flanked by flowers, bowls of water, candles, and brass incense holders. I remembered, as well, the words of a Greek Orthodox priest who spoke of the "otherness" of the priest as he approaches the altar. In this small chapel, in the fall of 1995, I was not alone. Zen and Orthodox priests crowded behind me. The Earth Altar sang its earth songs.

The light was brilliant; it shone on the altar and shone from within it. Edges blurred. I stood in the stillness, absorbed in the creative power of this little place. Nothing stirred. Sound faded. I was content and at peace. I felt right-sized. I needed to go after too few minutes. My son Willie was sharing the pulpit with the dean of the cathedral that day and I couldn't miss it. As I left, I glanced back briefly and saw a hand-lettered sign haphazardly attached to the iron-grated lattice work door. It said, "An Altar is a Place of Transformation."

We *are* building an altar at every moment. Every moment can be a moment of transformation if we can learn to live voluntarily. When the rush of traffic has your brain in a swirl, build an altar at the corner. When you are angry at your spouse, build an altar in the kitchen and breathe, in and out. When you see the devils, transform them. As you read on you will see how it has worked for me and for others and how it can work for you. There are altars at every turn when you know how to look for them.

As times change and the spiritual focus shifts, there are many recovering people who, like me, are looking for a more meaningful spiritual practice. Buddhist practice, Anglicanism, and AA are not the same, but they are not different. They share a common ground of awareness of suffering and the relief of suffering through persistent spiritual practice. Ordinary Recovery is just such a practice.

In a wonderful and paradoxical way, the gift of addiction is the possibility to walk the path of freedom from addiction. If I were not an addict, I could not be free.

Everyday life is the forge of freedom. Long-term freedom from addiction is not something that takes place outside of everyday life or only in Twelve Step meeting rooms, therapists' offices, or in occasional conversation with other recovering people. The freedom offered in Ordinary Recovery is not about "not drinking" but, rather, about the discovery of one's deep humanity. In Ordinary Recovery, imperfection is revealed and its delights are savored rather than despised. In the life of Ordinary Recovery, there is no self-disparaging talk of "defects of character," but, rather, a dedication to self-discovery, warts and all. Compassion is born from the ashes of isolation and recovery is happening in every moment. "One day at a time" includes Wednesdays.

I am writing from the inside out, as a recovered alcoholic and as a man with a spiritual life and longing that is as persistent, as present, and as deep as memories of my childhood days on the family farm near Medon, Tennessee. My spirit was nourished on that farm and when I awoke from the trance of alcohol addiction, I began to recover the questions and longings I had first known there. I am part red clay and part brown whiskey, with just a trace of temple incense.

I am a practicing Buddhist in the Mountain and Rivers

Order founded by the American Zen master John Daido Loori and in the Tiep Hien Order founded by Nobel nominee Thich Nhat Hanh. I am an Episcopalian as well and a member of the Cathedral of Saint John the Divine, heeding the advice of one of my teachers to come home to a childhood faith. I have found the practice of Buddhism "as I understand it" to be the motionless center of my recovery and, by extension, my entire life.

I am not alone. Members of the Haight Ashbury Generation were the first wave of a new and broader generation of people seeking help. We were raised during the era that saw the hyperbolic but affecting declaration of the death of God and that also saw the beginning of a new secularism. As Lenny Bruce said, "People are leaving the churches and looking for religion." The members of this generation are skeptical of "that old-time religion" but they want to sober up, and so are asking "Where am I in all of this?" We may be uncertain but we do know, gut deep, that some power greater than ourselves "which includes ourselves" has been revealed.

Ironically, both Zen Buddhism and Twelve Step programs insist on "ego reduction" as vital to sanity and awakening. I side with Frederick Franck in believing that sanity comes from ego *expansion*—an expansion so great that it includes, or better, embraces everyone and everything. This is a crucial distinction and well beyond what appears to be mere semantic snobbery, for addicts in the early months and even early years away from their drug. When I sobered up I didn't have an ego to reduce. I was pure id—all thirst and no self. Ordinary Recovery is the development of the embracing and compassionate self, the self without other, as in Whitman:

Self is everywhere, shining forth from all beings,
vaster than the vast, subtler than the most subtle,
unreachable, yet nearer than breath, than heartbeat.

Successful early recovery is universally marked by a
sense, however faint, of *enthusiasm* for a drug-free life. The
Greek word *enthousiasmos*, the root of enthusiasm, comes
from the adjective *entheos*, "having the god within." It is this
god within who inhabits these pages.

Coming Home

~~~~~~~~~~~~~~~~~~~~~~~~~~~~

*A religious awakening which does not awaken the sleeper to love
has roused him in vain.*

—JESSAMYN WEST

A LCOHOLISM IS THE DISEASE of living elsewhere. In active addiction, the present moment is a terrible and threatening place. The remorse for things done and the fear of what is to come crowd the eternal holy now into oblivion. There is no rest or comfort in the contemplation of the reality of the life of ongoing addiction. By the end of my addiction, the only escape from the horror of everyday life lay in the fragile amnesia of fantasy or illusion. Demons clawed at the windows in deep night. I awoke screaming from dreams of skeletal horses in dusty broken desert corrals, draped in rags of rotted flesh, grinning madly, empty eye sockets blazing ruby light. The throat is constricted in the real world. I had become a "hungry ghost"—the mythic creature with an enormous belly and pinprick mouth, cursed with an insatiable thirst. The thirst was too great. There was not enough liquor or cocaine or valium to slake it. There was no relief from the pain other than a little less pain. Life was slipping away unnoticed. The only sanity was in drunkenness.

During the last seven years of my active alcoholism, I never took a drink I enjoyed. During those seven years I had dry periods that lasted as long as three months, but for most of those years, as for the years previous, I was generally either drunk or detoxing every minute of the endless days. I would wake to a gray world outside my windows and not be sure if it was dusk or dawn. I was dis-spirited. When I came to in the morning, my first act was to hold my arms out to see which hand was shaking the most severely. Often the second was to see if I was alone.

Today I can see only a thin shadow of the true horror of those many years of addiction; I squint to see the wraith dancing awkwardly on a distant horizon. In my dreams, the hag in the pit at the bottom of the world looked up blindly to remind me of a life so far off center that, in waking time, I never knew a life could have a center. I lived in an ongoing state of emergency—a deep and ultimately sacred misery.

This is not alcoholism I am describing here. It is only my alcoholism. Yours may have been different. One dear friend of mine, dead many years now, came into AA when she went from three liqueurs a day to five. She was an attorney and had an active and admirable social life at the very top of New York social circles. She never did coke and left pills alone. She got "tipsy," not drunk. She was wise enough to see what so few can. She drank because she felt she needed to. It changed her and she longed for the changes. She stopped because she knew her reasoning was twisted. She quit when she was in her twenties and had been sober for over ten years when she died, a victim of terrorism.

My daughter quit drinking at the same age as my friend and has been sober for a long time now. Her story is not about liqueurs; hers is about vodka and drunk tanks and wrecked cars. She went down quicker than I did, and further. That she survived her early twenties is a blessing to all who know her. Her compassion today is as profound as her estrangement years ago. Her "elsewhere" was a long way away.

There is no one way to get to the end of this road. Whatever our own may be, it's bad enough.

When the enchantment ended, I was bewildered. I admitted, soul deep, that I was an alcoholic but I did not know what that was. I thought it had to mean something. By attending AA meetings I found what I needed to know. In meeting after meeting, I heard the same thing in many different words. In the richness of storytelling and open-hearted sharing, I found out what I always knew. Drinking causes suffering. Suffering causes drinking.

My dictionary says alcoholism is a "chronic, progressive pathological condition mainly affecting the nervous and digestive systems, caused by the excessive and habitual consumption of alcohol." Pathological. The mystery and ambiguity are put to an end in those five simple syllables for me. I am drawn to this definition not because of its clinical ring but out of a deeper resonance with the root word, *pathos*, from the Greek for suffering. Here was my core predicament. As active alcoholics we suffer alone in a savage state of denial and rage. As recovering alcoholics we still suffer, just as everyone does, but we do so in the company of other alcoholics and thus participate in a mutual antidote to suffering. The fact of compassion is realized. The dictionary defines compassion as a "deep awareness of the suffering of another coupled with the wish to relieve it." Compare the Twelfth Step of AA: "Having had a spiritual awakening as the result of these steps, we tried to

carry this message to alcoholics and to practice these principles in all our affairs." Compassion again. In Buddhism, the
opposite of greed, one of the Three Poisons, is compassion,
just as the opposites of the other poisons, anger and ignorance,
are wisdom and enlightenment. In the view of Buddhism, life
includes suffering and, through awakening to that fact and
awareness of the cause of suffering ("thirst" in some translations), we can put an end to suffering by following a path of
compassionate living. The First Step of AA—"We admitted
we were powerless over alcohol—that our lives had become
unmanageable"—is an awakening to the reality of suffering
and to its cause. That cause may be called existential greed or
it may be called a vast metabolic thirst, but it was the answer
to the central riddle of my life: Why couldn't I stop drinking?

I could not have stopped drinking alone. I tried, time and
again, only to fail. I have remained sober in large part by simply admitting that failure to others. Over many years of sobriety, I have relied on community for support and on story,
mine and others, for strength and growth. David Steindl-Rast,
a Benedictine monk who has had Zen training, says, "Religion
is personal, but it is not private."

I can neither commit myself to change nor provide comfort and support in solitude. It is not possible to practice religion alone. The word *religion* is from the Latin *religare*, to tie
fast or to connect (to the source). The source of my recovery
is in my Buddhist practice. The source of my Buddhist practice
is in my recovery. The deeper source is in my connection to
a community of fellow sufferers. Without community I would
die in virtual addiction, without drinking a drop. My isolation
and dread would damn me, as surely as a case of Smirnoff, to
a living death.

I did not come to community naturally. I was defiant and estranged. In the beginning of my recovery I wanted no part of it. I feared that I would be somehow "socialized," that what I had heard as a child—that one's sole purpose in life was to be a *productive* member of *society*—was in fact both true and inevitable. From an early age, with innocent and perfect intuition, I knew there must be more to it all than that.

I came of age in the fifties. By my early teenage years we lived in Coral Gables, Florida, and had moved on to Nashville, Tennessee by the time I was fifteen. We were churchgoers, Presbyterian mainly, and I still recall the aridity of Sunday School, where well-meaning adults taught us about responsibility while I wanted to hear about God; taught us the prevailing social wisdom while I wanted to hear about the mystic saints who roamed those myrrh-scented desert lands and sun-struck villages rich with olives and bread and clay vessels of water. I wanted to walk with those magical, wise, and peaceful men in the dust of the streets and sleep to dream God's dreams. Instead I was taught about "Christian Soldiers marching as to war, with the cross of Jesus going on before." With a soul-deep desire for parched Mediterranean lands, I was parched myself with a thirst that could not be slaked. Although I did not share the experience of my friend Sam who, living in the same part of the country, felt like an inhabitant of Judea rather than west Tennessee, I did at least know that something was missing.

My experience years later tells me that I was not alone. Friends have told me of their empty discontent from all those Sundays and of their guilt from feeling like the sole Pharisee in the land of the righteous. I was seeing something or the absence of something. With children of my own now, I have daily evidence, if I watch closely, that they, like me all those years ago, can sense fear and affectation and wonder what the hell is being covered up. Now I suspect that what I saw was the death of imagination. In imagination are the seeds of intimacy.

The fifties were the years of denial. A society that had seen too much war now wanted to see only peace. A growing economy, Bishop Sheen preaching about a world that did not contain evil, and the birth of consumerism as a leisure activity were the seeds not of the rebellion of the sixties but of the money-and-me decades yet to come. The world of imagination was deferred in favor of an overwrought pragmatism. Property became erotically charged and being happy was the apex of worldly success. When I poured whisky on top of this inculcated boondoggle, I lost my way. I became homeless.

By my late teens, I had learned to read the signs of feelings in others purely as a survival mechanism, because I could not fathom the reality of my own feelings. By my mid-twenties, after I had lost connection with my daughter, I lost connection with everyone. Imagination was replaced by cunning, creativity by imitation, and feelings by sentimentality. As I write these words my emotional jukebox is playing a phrase from Blind Faith: ". . . 'cause I'm wasted and I can't find my way home."

My mind was not sound, and by my thirties I was in a terrible world of random dependence. My unvoiced cry was, in the words of Joko Beck, "I want, I want I want . . . " with the deeper objective phrase ". . . the world to be my parents." By this time I paradoxically no longer wanted to drink. But I continued drinking, totally addicted, in and out of hospitals, a psychiatric ward, and a VA detox facility.

I am tempted to insert qualifying "howevers" and "nonethelesses" here to soften the picture I am painting, to create a chiaroscuro or weave a maze to dizzy you into misunderstanding how bad it was. I want you, that is, to be like I was, minimizing my condition by fooling myself into thinking my drunkenness was balanced by other factors in my life—a fool's yin yang. So, I will be direct. Not one person who knew me during my thirties ever said, "Oh, it wasn't that bad."

By my late thirties, my dreams were night terrors and my waking life, in Bill Wilson's piquant phrase, was one of "anxious apartness." It is only small comfort to say that during those years and to this day it was not necessary to be an alcoholic to be numb; cunning, imitation, and sentimentality were, are, epidemic. My emotional flatness was costly, and I continue to pay. Although my story and the stories of many alcoholics are microcosmic, I avoid, when I can, the inflation that comes from over-identification with the culture at large. Being part of sickness does not excuse it.

Thich Nhat Hanh says, "The root of war is how we live our daily lives." In many petty ways, I was at war for thirty years. On June 24th, 1984, I declared peace by surrendering. I admitted in my deepest self that I was alcoholic. The Twelve steps of Alcoholics Anonymous lead, by Steps Eleven and Twelve, to ongoing efforts to "improve" conscious contact with a power greater than ourselves and to an admission of a spiritual awakening. That conscious contact and that awakening of the spirit began for me, however primitively, on that day. Shortly afterward, I made a promise to myself to spend the rest of my life with peaceful people. I have been blessed to see that promise, fitfully, bear fruit.

Off the Cushion and
Out the Door

~~~~~~~~~~~~~~~~~~~~~~~~

BREATHING ROOM

THERE IS A SMALL ROOM in my basement that we call the "breathing room." The idea and poetic name came from Thich Nhat Hanh in his wonderful book *The Miracle of Mindfulness*. I am married and there are four children living at home, along with three adopted Labrador retrievers and two cats. This is a busy place. Sometimes, it's like living in a monastery; more often it's like living in a saloon. We all care for each other very much. Care for each other, that is, except when one or another of us might like to see some other one of us leaving on a long journey to some unimaginably uninteresting place. "So long. Take your time. Can I have your desk?" Tempers flare in our home just like in yours and everyone's. It's in relationship that we find our edges.

Therefore, we built the breathing room.

The room itself is small, about ten feet by ten feet, and was patched together in the back of the basement furnace room. Two walls are made of concrete blocks and the other two of Sheetrock. There is a small table with some beautiful objects—an altar of the present moment. One of the objects on that table is a large *rin* gong, a bell six inches in diameter resting on a colorful cushion, with a small padded stick for ringing. In Vietnamese, a bell is not "struck" but "invited" to ring. In formal practice, the bell master first touches the rim of the bell with this padded stick, the "inviter," in order to awaken the bell. The stick is held to the rim, producing a "thunk." Then the bell is invited to ring with a full "strike," with the inviter quickly pulled back. That is how the bell is sounded in our home.

There is some simple art on the walls of our breathing room and there is another smaller table with an incense burner, matches, and sticks of incense. There is no trace of religious iconography, yet the room has the feel of a sacred place. There are cushions only, no chairs and no other furniture.

When strife begins, anyone who is a partner to it can go to the breathing room, invite the bell to ring, light incense, and then sit quietly, following his breath and returning to the present moment. Thoughts of unfairness and resentment are noticed and gently dismissed. This is not so difficult. When the resentment comes up, just say "Thank you for sharing," and let it go. The mind is brought back to the breath. Our house is small enough, and the bell and incense insistent enough, that we all know when someone is in the room inviting peace for everyone else. When we hear the sound of the bell or smell the pungent incense, we are all reminded to return to the present moment and put aside our petty grievances. Anyone who wishes may go down to the room, invite the bell as well, and join in the practice of the present moment. This is a most healing practice. I encourage you to make a breathing room of your own. It has made such an important difference in our exuberant family.

All you need is the space and a few beautiful objects to help you to return to the present moment. I strongly urge you to invest in a bell and, if you like it, some incense. If you do not have a room to use as a breathing room, you can designate any quiet corner for this use. "Breathing room" is a state of mind more than a place. Bonnie Myotai Treace, Sensei, says, "If you are free, it doesn't matter where you put the furniture."

It is also possible, in that spirit, to return to your breathing room at any moment.

This calligraphy represents the ideogram for *mindfulness*. I keep one much like it on the wall over my desk. The top element means "now" and has its origins in a pictograph in the shape of a sheltering roof. This roof implies inclusiveness or covering. The lower element means both "heart" and "mind." In Eastern countries "heart" and "mind" are not separate. You can see that the shape of the lower element is that of a heart with three chambers.

The ideogram taken as a whole can be translated as "being full-hearted right now," and, according to the calligrapher, author, and activist Kazuaki Tahahashi, other translations include "to have something at heart," "to keep on remembering," "to chant," and "to pray." As a noun, it means "thought," "sense," "wish," "concern," and finally "mindfulness." So to be mindful is to have the heart/mind fully focused on the present moment. There is nothing extra. There is nothing lacking. When we are mindful, we are showing up for our lives. An ancient master said that one who lives in forgetfulness, dies in a dream. Thich Nhat Hanh says that to live mindfully is "to keep our appointment with life." When the flower blooms, we see it. When our partner is suffering, we see it. Our heart/ mind is fully present for all things and activities.

You will find this ideogram throughout the rest of this book. When you come upon it, please take some time to breathe in and out and return to the place of safe dwelling, the present moment. Kazuaki Tanahashi has drawn the ideograms especially for this book. Look carefully. Each of them is unique. Mindfulness is not a static practice. Mindfulness at fifty-fourth Street and Seventh Avenue in New York has a different quality from mindfulness on Lacey Road outside of Medon, Tennessee. When you come upon Kaz's beautiful drawings, look at them with your entire attention. What do they suggest to you? How are they different? How are they the same? I feel privileged to have the gift of Kaz's art for this book. Treat them with respect and consideration. Consider them carefully.

There is time to do this. I don't mean for you to rush through this book. We all need some breathing room. Sometimes the ideogram is followed by thoughts or suggestions headed "Breathing Room." These are offered as exercises in mindfulness in everyday life. Here is where we can take the spirit of the breathing room into the world. Please use them. At other times, no specific breathing room suggestions are given. In those cases, use the ideogram to just take a moment to focus on the present. Ask yourself where your feet are. Where are your hands and how do your legs feel right now? Take this time for yourself when you see the mindfulness ideogram. Remind yourself whose life this is.

My Liver, My Mind, My Self

Y OU HAVE PROBABLY HEARD that alcoholism is considered a disease of body, mind, and spirit. I don't think that means it is about getting drunk, stupid, and silent. It seems to be more about a screwed-up liver and a bewildered mind. Spirit is the victim.

Here is the definition of the liver from the *Columbia Encyclopedia*.

> liver: largest glandular organ of the body. It lies on the right side of the abdominal cavity, beneath the diaphragm, and is made up of four unequal lobes. Liver tissue consists of thousands of tiny lobules, in turn made up of hepatic cells, the basic metabolic cells. The liver is thought to perform over 500 functions involving the digestive system, excretion, blood chemistry and detoxification, and the storage of vitamins and minerals. Of the liver's many digestive system functions, the production of bile (for fat digestion) and storage of glucose (see glycogen) are particularly important.

My liver doesn't work right. If you are an alcoholic, neither does yours. Here is what my liver did when I poured alcohol into it. Once my daily hit of brandy and beer slipped past the paroxysm in my throat and the shiver in my face, it traveled to the liver to be processed and disposed of. A healthy liver robs the alcohol of its ability to create havoc—the toxic properties are leavened by chemical reactions. First the alcohol becomes acetaldehyde, which is converted to acetate that is then broken down into carbon dioxide and water and is eliminated by urinating, sweating, and breathing. When I drank and you smelled the booze on my breath, it was my liver at work. But here is the break point, the source of my misery and the end of poetry: My liver has an inherited liver enzyme abnormality that inhibits the normal process of metabolism. The two principal enzymes, alcohol dehydrogenase (ADH) and acetaldehyde dehydrogenase (ALDH), vary in small ways in the livers of alcoholics. In addition, there are two liver metabolites, 2,3-butanediol and 1,2-propanediol, that are present only in alcoholics' livers. If you are an alcoholic, you've *probably* got them, and if you're not, you *definitely* don't. The end result of all this is that my liver has devised an alternate way of metabolizing alcohol, known as microsomal ethanol oxidating system (MEOS). This means that my liver is better at processing alcohol into acetaldehyde than a normal liver. That's the good news. The bad news is that my liver is less efficient at eliminating it than it is at producing it. Toxicity happens. When I drank the lights grew mellower, the music was softer, people seemed gentler and wiser, and I couldn't find my way home.

Why is it, then, that I couldn't just quit? I could. I quit daily. I quit daily, never to drink again. I quit daily, only to drink again. I thought that I could beat this thing. This thing was outside of me.

When I was an editor at Harper San Francisco, I had occasion to spend some time with Gregory Bateson at the Esalen Institute in Big Sur. I was in awe of this massive man with his gentle smile and shimmering eyes. I read every word that he had written and was mystified by most of it. I suspect that his book *Steps to an Ecology of Mind* joins a short list of unread, endlessly chatted about works of great importance. But Gregory's book and his short paper "The Cybernetics of 'Self': A Theory of Alcoholism" grabbed me and wouldn't let go. True enough, I kept a bottle of Dry Sack in my desk drawer, a bottle of vodka in my car, and a handful of loose Valium in my shirt pocket, so any value I drew from this paper was in its aid to my denial. I could after all quote Bateson on epistemology and cybernetics and Eastern ways of thinking and then, with a knowing nod, let you know that *I* was not one of *them*. Consider how difficult it is—what a skill it is—to be condescending to one's self! Nonetheless, I couldn't get that essay out of my mind. I now know that although I didn't get the meaning of it, there was a part of me that knew it contained an important answer to my central question: *What's wrong?*

Now I understand the phenomena of "alcoholic denial" and "alcoholic pride" as just this epistemological dilemma that I was living. *I,* this separate self, was not one of *them*. My little, distinct "self" was one thing and alcoholism was some other thing, outside of me. Denial was not a matter of disavowal or avoidance of real information. It was an epistemological dilemma. "Stinking thinking," in the words of AA hardliners, was the real culprit. Socially I was blamed for my drinking and, socially, I was expected to use "will-power" to overcome it. And every time I tried and failed I was more bewildered. The dark ordinariness of it got me down. Concurrently alcoholic pride drove me on. Bateson writes of this pride as not a pride in achievement or accomplishment but as an obsessive acceptance of a challenge. I didn't say "I did it!" but "I can do it." When I failed I thought, "I can't be an alcoholic. She's an alcoholic and I'm not like her." The liturgy was this: "I can" followed by "I'm not."

There was also a deadly coda on those few occasions when I did manage to do without liquor or cocaine for over three days. Rather than "I did," it remained "I can." More perversely, it was "I did it once, I can do it again. Let's have just one." I had met one challenge, not drinking, so now I could face a greater one—controlling my drinking. I can drink safely, I said. But I cannot drink safely, so the battle is joined again. It is this imaginary me, separate from everything, that can beat this thing, alcoholism, that is out there somewhere. This is the mind's idea and it is peculiarly Western. What I didn't get and what the vast majority of people don't get is that the disease is not in the bottle, it is in the drinker. And alcoholism is the only disease where the symptom, excessive drinking, is fatal.

So when "I" gave up, what really happened? I surrendered. Surrender has been described variously as a functional acceptance of reality on an unconscious level, a huge emotional displacement and re-arrangement, or a miracle. I like "miracle," but Bateson forces me to accept "epistemological shift." What happened was this. Rather than me changing my mind, my mind changed. Bateson writes of "the difference that makes a difference," that bit of information in a system that as it works in the system also changes it. An accumulation of "bits" absorbed over time led me from "I can" to "I am." The isolated "self" was revealed. Just as in Zen, "body and mind fell away." "To study the self is to forget the self. To forget the self is to be enlightened by the 10,000 things." The promise of the Eighth Step of Alcoholics Anonymous is that "this is the beginning of the end of isolation from our fellows and from God." My experience is otherwise. This "functional acceptance of reality on an unconscious level" marked that beginning. I was no longer able to see myself as separate. The question became, "How far could I go in dissolving those boundaries?" Any member of AA is familiar with the fear-filled expression, "the hole in the center of the doughnut." The implied question is, "Will I disappear?" There are two answers. You already are the hole in the center of the doughnut. To the question of disappearing, the answer is "just look around you." Some of the most vividly distinctive people in my viewfinder are some of the most deeply spiritual and compassionate.

When the construct of years of drinking crumbled, I saw that my liver got my mind to lie and the illusion of "self" just deepened the deception. The problem was epistemology. The only reality in the whole damned equation is a malfunctioning liver. It's important to understand this if we are to understand the fallacy of the defective, endlessly recovering alcoholic. There is not much romance left and not much blame either. Liver and occidental mind led me to that dismal room in the Chelsea Hotel.

If you have already caught alcoholism and think that your liver is just fine, thank you, and that you never really denied your alcoholism, don't let this idea of mine influence you. If you're not sure if you're alcoholic, the same goes.

The real definition of my alcoholism is that when I drink, my life goes down the toilet. How about you?

Mindfulness

~~~~~~

GOD AND THE ORDINARY

ONE OF MY TEACHERS TOLD ME that the way of Zen is the way of knowing God, that is, of knowing the power of things as they are. The Zen teacher Robert Aitken tells the story of a member of his community who was in treatment for alcoholism and who was bewildered by what seemed to be this insistence that he believe in creator God or, in the AA phrase, a power "greater than ourselves" who will restore us to sanity. What was he to do, as a Buddhist? Aitken Roshi pointed out of the hospital window at the Ko'olau Mountains. There they were, these fire-breathing mountains, towering over the landscape, rich with the power of things-as-they-are.

When I read this story in Aitken's translation of *The Gateless Barrier*, an essential collection of Zen koans and commentaries, I could see those powerful mountains declaring themselves. I understood then the idea of a power greater than myself. It was just this power of things-as-they-are. How marvelous. I could see this power everywhere I looked! I didn't need to go to church to see God. She was in the palm of my hand or in the curl of my son's hair, wet in the bath.

Lynda Sexson says, "Overcoming a dualistic heritage (however strongly those dualistic presuppositions seem to belong to religious knowledge) brings one into the sphere in which ordinary reality is saturated with the sacred." Then, curiously resonant with Shunryu Suzuki, she goes on: "Religion is made up of *nothing special* [emphasis added]—the ordinary is holy or potentially holy; since the object of the religious is no-thing, its images can be improvised from oatmeal boxes and sand sculpture." Transformation becomes reality and the whole earth shines with the power of things as they are. When Carl Jung was asked if he believed in God, he said no, that he knew God. This ongoing relationship with God is immediately available; it is, in fact, *only* immediately available.

How do we get there? If we are immersed in the sacred, how do we learn to see it, touch it, know it? How does God become flesh? The answer is mindfulness.

According to Thich Nhat Hanh, mindfulness is the "energy that sheds light on all things and all activities, producing the power of concentration, bringing forth deep insight and awakening." I am particularly struck by one example that Thay, as he is known, gives of a lack of mindfulness. He says that if a teacher notices that a student has slammed a door rather than closing it quietly, he will know that the student is not practicing mindfulness. Closing the door quietly is not mindfulness. Mindfulness is knowing that you are closing the door quietly.

This example reminds me of an incident early in my own Zen training. I had rushed from the meditation hall with the other students to sit outside the door of the dharma room, the room of teaching, to wait to be called for dokusan, which is face-to-face teaching or interview, with my teacher Daido.

When my turn came, I hurled myself into the room. Properly, I did one full bow with the student who was still in the room after completing her interview. She left, closing the door noiselessly. I then stepped sideways to a position facing the teacher, seated powerfully on his cushion. I hurriedly bowed three more times and then sat in seiza, a particularly painful position where the legs are folded double and the butt rests on the heels. I told Daido my name, as is usual, and then asked the question that was eating me up. It is neither appropriate nor necessary to tell it here. Daido answered and went on to say that I was a ball of fractured energy coming through his door. He strongly recommended that I sit zazen more often, longer, and with deeper concentration. I mumbled my assent. He asked if there was anything else and when I muttered "no" he rang the bell that ends each session and signals the next student to come in. Then, just as I was about to stand, he very offhandedly and gently pointed out that I had bowed too many times when I came into the room. He explained the proper sequence while I hovered, half kneeling, half standing. I muttered something again and hobbled off. On the way out, I slammed the door. I can still hear it.

What follows is an exercise in mindfulness which is extremely popular with the people who attend Ordinary Recovery retreats.

How to Cook Brown Rice
(With Gratitude to Edward Espe Brown)

You will need a cast iron pot with a heavy lid. A good one costs about as much as a bottle of single malt scotch. If the lid is not heavy enough to create a seal, you may put a brick or some other heavy weight on top of it. This is important. If the lid fits poorly, steam will escape. If you must, cover the pot with foil. Then put the lid on and weight it down.

You will need good, high quality rice. If possible, buy it at a natural foods store. There are four types of brown rice: short grain, medium grain, long grain, and sweet rice. For normal use, either short grain or medium grain is best. Long grain can be mixed with other rices in more elaborate dishes than the one we are cooking here. Sweet rice is, well, sweet and delicious. It is highly glutinous and very high in protein. For this recipe, use one cup of short or medium grain rice.

You will need water and salt. The water should be pure. The salt should be sea salt, if possible.

First, clean the cast iron pot carefully. While you are cleaning the pot, concentrate all your energy on the task. Clean this pot as if the salvation of the planet depended on it. Perhaps it does. Clean it with water as hot as you can stand— the hotter the better—and just the right amount of soap, which is probably far less than you think. Use your bare hand to clean the pot and as you swirl the hot soapy water around, pay attention to the sensation of the water and the surface of the pot. Breathe gently and easily. Smile a half smile as you wash the pot. Take time. Remember the pot is only going to get dirty again. Clean it well. Try to do nothing other than cleaning the pot. Breathe and smile. Rinse the pot thoroughly and carefully wipe it dry.

Now it's time to clean the rice. Move directly to this step when the pot is dry. There is plenty of time to cook this brown rice. Cook it as if there were no time for anything else. Cook it as if there were nothing other than cooking it. Cooking brown rice begins long before the water is hot or the rice is clean. It does not begin at the store where you bought it. Does it begin in the rice fields? While you are cleaning the rice, consider when this rice-cooking, that is now nearly over, began. First put the rice on a large plate. Pick over it and remove any stones, clumps of dirt, or other impurities. This dirt, how did it come to your plate? Put the picked-over rice in the dry pot. Pour in enough water to cover it. Swirl the rice and water around with your hand. Feel the tiny grains against your fingers. The water will color. Pour the water into a container for watering plants or some other use. Wash the rice two or three more times or until the water is nearly clear, each time saving the water.

Now rinse the rice in a colander or strainer, quickly and carefully. Shake it until most of the water is gone. Breathe. Smile.

Put the rice back in the pot. Add two cups of cool water. Wait for one hour. Add a pinch of sea salt. Breathe and smile. Regard the rice in the pot. How did it come to be there? Metaphysics are not optional. It is also a good idea to add a tablespoon of butter or oil now. Turn up the heat to high and bring the rice to a furious boil. Watch the change as the boiling point approaches. The water becomes agitated and there seem to be areas of greater and lesser movement. The melted butter forms patterns on the moving surface. When a full boil is reached, the activity seems relentless and chaotic. Turn the heat to low and cover the pot. Breathe and smile.

Cook the rice for one hour.

Do not open the pot. Be patient. It is very important not to open it. Use this time for yourself. Do not be "entertained." Turn off the TV, radio, and stereo. Is it possible to be silent for this entire sixty minutes?

Toward the end of the hour, listen carefully to the pot. A bubbling sound means the rice is still cooking. If there is a sound of crackling, the rice is cooked and is toasting. Trust your senses. If it's crackling, turn the heat off even if the hour is not up.

Do not open the pot until just before serving. Fluff the rice with a couple of forks.

Breathe.

Eat the rice slowly. Consider how it came to you. Consider, in the words of the Zen teacher and cook Ed Brown, how it becomes you.

Taste your rice deeply.

Psychedelic Cheeseburgers and Shimmering Pines

~~~~~~~~~~~~~~~~~~~~~~~~~~~~~~~~

B ACK IN THE MID-TO-LATE SIXTIES, I tended bar and hung out in Tampa, Florida. The bar where I spent the most time was a magnet for the One Percenters, a motorcycle gang modeled after the Hell's Angels, and was a hippie, student, and local redneck lush hangout. We served beer, sandwiches, and hamburgers, which I generally grilled while testing the latest exotic hallucinogen, prior to marketing, for a friend in retail. Later in the evening, in many cases, I wouldn't be able to make sense out of a handful of change. The beer was provided by a sinister family, the security by the One Percenters, and the harassment by Malcolm Beard and the Hillsborough County Sheriff's Department. Only one person was shot on my watch; the fights were brutal and quickly ended. Just three couples had sex during business hours, and the fellow who masturbated by the billiard table was finally permanently 86ed.

This bar and the two that had preceded it, only to be burned down in mysterious circumstances, were high energy spots. They smelled of sour beer, fried fat, cigarettes, Pine-sol, and sweat. There was a sign over the urinal in the men's room that read, "Please don't eat the big white mints," and the graffiti in the women's room was from *Quiet Days in Clichy*. It read "A good meal, a good talk, a good fuck. What better way to spend the day. There were no worms devouring her conscience." On the door to the men's room someone had scrawled "POLYMORPHOUS PERVERSITY!" as if the phrase had meaning just by looming large and alone in this juicy little roadhouse. The men I knew who were regulars there talked like W. C. Fields, their words squeezed through the glottis, rolled across a thickened tongue, and oozed out of the side of the mouth, with key words elongated and whinnied. "I'd like a Beeeer, Billy me lad." These were wonderful, dark times; I regret little of what happened during those years. I am also certain that to paint them with either too light or too dark a brush is deadly.

After nearly forty years without any contact between us, I had a long e-mail conversation with one of my best friends from elementary grades through our sophomore year of high school. We shared our histories with each other, only to find that our lives could not have been more different. During my years in Tampa, and for many to follow, Carlton was living a life of responsibility and probity. He finished college in three years and completed graduate school in due course soon thereafter. Like me, he did his time in the Army, but he served in an intellectual's position in the Signal Corps while I was an infantry officer and paratrooper. He later went into business while I descended into alcoholic madness. He married and stayed married while I was twice divorced before finally meeting a woman who was not my type, thank God. My old friend and I love each other for who we are, not for what we have done or failed to do. My lesson, then, in renewing this wonderful friendship is to treat myself as Carlton treats me: "Perfect and complete, lacking nothing."

There is a central, damaging anomaly at the core of the

AA model of recovery from addiction that haunted me for a long time. It is a haywire troublemaker for people trying to get sober, most often driving them away, and an ongoing vexation for those who are able to stick with abstinence in spite of it. If you're like me, and hung out in your equivalent of that funky roadhouse in Tampa and maybe did more than your fair share of deeply naughty business, you want to be as careful not to fall into the blame trap as to fall into the I-couldn't-help-it trap. The problem is this.

In AA literature and in meeting rooms worldwide, alcoholism is first defined as a disease, "an allergy of mind and body," and then the alcoholic is implicitly *blamed* for having it. The blame is in the insistence that alcoholics are less whole or moral than "normies" or "earth people"—such pitiable sobriquets, so damning in their polarizing meanness—and that we suffer from crippling "defects of character" and chronic inabilities to form relationships with others, which characteristics *"made* alcoholics of us in the first place" (emphasis added). The Twelve Steps speak of "moral" inventories, "defects of character," and "shortcomings," and the literature of AA tells us that we are less able to handle anger than other people and are "grandiose and immature in the extreme."

It is easy enough to argue that this is all simply a matter of language. It *is* simply a matter of language and in this case the language is damaging. I came to accept as true the story about myself that I learned through AA, with all its implicit judgments, no matter how false it is. I was convinced that I was bad rather than sick. Theory of disease or powerlessness, doesn't mean much to someone who is newly sober. When we finally see the light, it can nearly blind us. Living in the light is terrifying. Community and story form our conceptions of ourselves in the beginning. Like children who are criticized, we think poorly of ourselves. Even when we are told that we are not "bad people getting good" but are "sick people getting well," we are still hearing that there is something wrong with us. It is my experience that wrong/right, sick/well, bad/good as they apply to my self are injurious. I am what I am at any particular moment, drunk or sober.

This judgemental attitude is easy to understand. The two principal books of AA, the "Big Book" (properly *Alcoholics Anonymous*) and the "12 and 12" (properly *Twelve Steps and Twelve Traditions*), although hardly old books, were written several decades ago and reflect the trends and tempers and prejudices of their milieu. No matter how hard the founders and their brothers and (so few) sisters tried to insist on the disease model, the moralizing judgements of generations blocked their way. That judgement that alkies are "at fault" persists to this day. "You have a disease and you are wrong for having it. Shame on you!"

I recently heard a speaker in an AA meeting identify himself this way: "I am an alcoholic and my *problem* is Bill." (Not his real name). That was not the first time I have heard such a statement nor will it be the last. My skin crawls every time I hear it. At a deeper level, I am saddened when I hear such self-hatred. I identify with it, of course. Toward the end of my active addiction, I felt flawed and ill-made, a sloppy construction with vital pieces tossed willy-nilly on the workshop floor. So I understand what the speaker meant in saying that in his life he was the problem. I empathize with him and I wish him no harm. However, I think we need to look more closely at this understanding. When a man says that he is a problem he is saying that he is an object. When he becomes an object, somehow outside of himself, he is committing a violent act upon himself that encourages further violence. This attitude of violence to the self is pervasive in AA. The wheel of the dis-spirited life continues to spin.

In Buddhism, we speak of *ahimsa*, which means nonviolence. It has become my aspiration to practice ahimsa in my life of recovery and my life after recovery. It is not so easy. Nonviolence to the self is not supported by the overt culture of our times and is only slightly less denigrated by the "sober minority." "Over there is me, defective and always coming up short. But I'm working on it." As long as I drank and used drugs but saw that behavior as a problem outside of me, a problem that would crumble before my separate will, I stayed drunk. Similarly, in my sober life, as long as I think I am the trouble, I will stay troubled. As long as I think I am the problem, my life will be problematic. The practice of ahimsa, nonviolence, directed toward myself will lead to a practice of nonviolence to earth, God, and other. It is in setting up these judgements about myself that I become violent and ineffectual.

I am not the problem. The problem is in me, but it is not me. But just as the problem is not me, it is also *not* not me. I contain it. Just as I am not a problem named Bill, I am also not an alcoholic named Bill. I often hear people identify themselves in AA meetings by saying, "I'm an alcoholic and my name is——," reversing the traditional greeting ("My name is——and I'm an alcoholic"). I don't think this helps. It has the effect of saying either that my whole identity is determined by a deviant liver or, more insidiously, that I am the "real" alcoholic in this room, apart from and better than the rest of you. Alcoholism is contained by me, but it is not me.

I'm a father, a husband, a Buddhist, a white Anglo-Saxon male over fifty, all of it. I've got it, but I'm not it. This is an important understanding. Alcoholism is not separate from me, but I am not alcoholism. The problem is not separate from me, but I am not the problem. Moreover, alcoholism is not the problem.

If alcoholism is a disease and I've got it, but am not wrong for having it, then why am I such a mess? Which is the chicken and where is the egg? Is a disease the excuse for my life lying in ruins around my feet or is it the reason? What is this alcoholism that caused me to lose the affection of my family and the ability to work successfully? Is it so that my liver's inability to metabolize ACTH caused my heart to harden?

After many years without alcohol and drugs, I came to the conclusion that I needed finally to accept that my problem might be lack of will power, character, and courage. Maybe I was just a bad person, getting worse. I also came to understand that I might have a genetic disorder that manipulated me, at its whim, into a condition of sorrow and hopelessness that I would not wish upon anyone. Here's the reality. Alcoholism is in me like grey eyes and bad teeth. It doesn't matter a whit, ultimately, whether I got it from Dad or my own inability not to bite the other children.

Chicken and egg are one. No cause, no effect. No inside, no outside. No me, separate from my illness.

So what about the "sick alcoholic," willful in the extreme, plagued by insecurity and fear, grandiose and self-loathing—"the asshole at the center of the universe" or Jung's King Baby? All of those negative traits are mine. I am grandiose, naive, and quick to anger. So are most of the people I know, alcoholic or not. I am also able to see my place in the scheme of things, to be aggressive and hard-minded, to act out of compassion and understanding. Siegfried Sassoon said, "In me the tiger sniffs the rose."

So, rather than being either defective because of genes or gin, or perfect because of Buddhism and recovery programs, I discover that I am merely human.

In trying to live a spiritual life, I learn to identify those traits that in their darkness do great harm. I don't have to look too far. Greed, aversion, and ignorance show up in my everyday life; I don't need to read the sutras to identify my "sins." I understand sin as a "condition of estrangement" from God as a result of my actions or, better, as a result of my greed, aversion, and ignorance. When I awoke from all those years of drunkenness and first began to sense my connectedness, I was seeing my sinfulness, my estrangement from God and from self, earth, and other. Today I know at some profound level that there is no difference among the four. I also know that my wife is not myself, that Hurricane Mountain in the Adirondacks is a place I go to, out there, and that God lives in my wife and in Hurricane Mountain.

My "defects of character" are never going to be miraculously taken away. My hope and, in some cases, my experience is that I can wear them out by the "fire of attention," as Joko Beck describes it.

Who among us is not sick? Sicker than thou is a dangerous game. I do not consider myself to be "defective." I also do not see my drunken past as evidence of an eternally rotten character. However, contrary to AA dogma, I do regret some parts of my past. I am not able to excuse or rationalize them. I did some terrible things. I watched my daughter wave to

46/

me, her tiny hand out the window, as she and her mother drove off to another state to live. I waved back and would not feel. I went into my shabby stucco house on the outskirts of Tampa and drank myself sick. I regret the tears I would not shed that day and the words I didn't say. I have made my peace with that day and with the person I was on that day, but I can't help but wish I had been a better and stronger man.

In Buddhist psychology we talk of *alaya-vijnana*, or "storehouse consciousness" as that place where the seeds of all psychological phenomena are stored. The seeds of anger and the seeds of understanding are there, waiting to be watered. I first heard this idea explained by Thich Nhat Hanh in the dharma hall in Plum Village. I retain to this day the music of his voice and the gentle image of a seedbed in green crinkled cardboard, loamy and rich, filled with tiny green seeds, somehow tucked away in my belly. I am grateful that my mind is so childishly simple, at least when it's time to visualize.

I have not answered my own question. Why this troubling bind of inevitability and guilt? It is this. Research done in the 1980s has proven that there is no such critter as an "alcoholic personality" *before* the onset of drinking. The most significant study was done by Dr. George Vaillant of Harvard University. This was a "natural history," a longitudinal study of 660 men whose lives were studied over a period of forty years, from 1940 until 1980. Of those who became alcoholic, the study showed that there were absolutely no common personality or behavioral factors that could have reliably predicted their illness before its onset.

The so-called alcoholic personality is spawned by the appetite of the illness. What I did, I did in service to my malfunctioning liver. That's not a very romantic conclusion. Even seeing my alcoholism as the dark twin, as useful as it is, is diminished a bit when I realize that my irritated liver is the real villain here. Not much poetry in that. Alcoholism is pretty ordinary—not a spiritual search, not a moral weakness, not even "the good man's weakness." Just the ordinary and unremarkable function of a maladjusted liver.

You and I are fascinated by alcoholism because we've got it. The larger society is fascinated by it because our behavior, in its thrall, often pushes some distant limits. Chronic psoriasis doesn't lead to any place very interesting. We can be signposts to fascinating places that other folks would just as soon not visit. These are dark gardens we grow in.

The lotus flower blooms best from the mud. All that I did in those years of darkness led to this moment right here.

In 1991, I got a phone call from the head monk of Zen Mountain Monastery. He was calling to tell me that I had been accepted to begin the arduous journey toward becoming a member of the Mountain and Rivers Order and a student of Abbot John Daido Loori. This monk, Shugen, and I talked for several minutes and he outlined the barrier gates to admission as a full-time student that I had yet to pass through. This included an all-day sit, called *tangaryo,* when applicants sit zazen from before dawn until sunset with only a forty-five minute break for lunch. There is also an informal tea with the Abbot and a more intimate face-to-face interview when the aspiring student formally requests to be accepted as a student.

This conversation took place on a morning in the early spring. Trees were green again and the breeze was sweet. When Shugen and I had finished talking, I went for a walk. The light was brighter and the trees were greener than they had any right to be. The rich earth cushioned my step. I breathed the spring air deeply. Just then, a line of geese flew overhead. Their sudden cries were like a Zen master's explosive shout or like the slap of the monitor's stick on the shoulders of a meditator slipping into sleep. I woke up and for a moment disappeared into pine and new breeze and goose honk. The pines shimmered their welcome. Body and mind had fallen away and for a moment I had come back to my true self. The next step in my full recovery had been taken and the great earth was witness.

Such moments are fleeting and I am grateful to have been awake to notice it. You cannot induce such moments. You must be awake and alert to see them.

The lotus blooms best from the mud. All those greasy psychedelic cheeseburgers had led directly to the place of shimmering pines. I was and am neither "good" nor "bad." "All of us," my teacher says, "are perfect and complete, exactly as we are, lacking nothing."

Making Stew

~~~~~~~~~~~~~~~~~~~~~~~~~

J OAN HALIFAX SAYS that if "we look deeply into ourselves we can see that our basic nature is free of suffering,
that our lives are wholesome and complete." We are free
of the suffering of delusion. We do not believe that we are
defective or inadequate. The self is seen as "me and the world
I live in." How could such a wondrous thing be defective? We
are only human. When you start to hear too much about
"defects," do this: Consider stew.

Here are the ingredients for Tofu Miso Stew from *The
Tassajara Recipe Book* by Edward Espe Brown: onions, dark
sesame oil, carrots, celery ribs, burdock root, fresh mush-
rooms, a yam, daikon or turnip, a potato, garlic, ginger, barley
flour, more sesame oil, red miso, light sesame oil, tofu, scallions, cilantro, soy sauce, and Sichuan pepper. This is a wonderful stew. It is fragrant and rich with subtlety.

If I invited you to make this stew with only this list of
ingredients, you would probably have a very hard time of it.
How much sesame oil? How many onions? Do I sauté them?
The more practiced cooks might be able to make a go of it
while those who have no cooking practice would go hungry.

It is a question of balance. If you put in a cup of the
Sichuan pepper, the stew would be ruined. If you put in too
little cilantro, the result would be bland and of little interest;
too much and it would steal your breath. Without just the
right amount of soy, the taste of burdock and celery ribs is

not fully realized. If the scallions are overcooked or the potatoes are undercooked, the stew tastes either burned or raw.
The stew, we can say, is perfect and complete, *lacking nothing,*
just as it is. But without the careful hand of the cook balancing
the ingredients just so, it is unrealized.

Where would you be without every one of your precious
ingredients? Is stubbornness a defect when you are determined not to light another cigarette or eat another donut? Is
anger a defect when you are falsely accused? Ingredients are
what they are; they just need to be used judiciously.

We see that the idea of "defects of character" has no
place in Ordinary Recovery. You can use the term *ingredients*
as I suggest here, a suggestion that comes from Bernard Tset-
sugen Glassman, an American Zen teacher and dharma

brother of my teacher Daidoshi. You can also find a word that works for you. This is important. I would be pleased to hear from you. What word is it that works without being negative and judgmental? Please send it to me in care of my publisher.

There is something else you can do to get away from this defective business. If you cook and have a favorite recipe, you are a little ahead of the game. If you do not cook, find some simple recipe for something that looks satisfying to you. Cook this dish mindfully whenever you find yourself on a run of self-negating talk. Take some time and cook it when you've been in a situation where there is too much of this destructive talk. As you cook it, consider each ingredient and see how they make the dish work. What would it be like without this ingredient? With too much? Too little? You can express your gratitude to the pepper and bow to the salt.

By the way, there is no such thing as too much garlic.

Stepping Off the
Hundred-Foot Pole

~~~~~~~~~~~~~~~~~~~

THE END OF RECOVERY

THE WORD *RECOVERY* is a metonym that sets off lots of alarms—a buzzword that often connotes selfishness, whiny claims of victimization, and endless dependence and juvenile irresponsibility. For some, it also suggests a worldwide network of people, a community of fellow sufferers who support each other in the task of overcoming disease or misfortune. For some, it's about Oprah, while for others it's about quiet service. For some, it's an excuse for inaction and for others a call to a love without questions or judgments. As you read on I ask that you read with the alarms shut down.

I consider recovery to be *a process that ends.* You will see that when recovery ends in a spiritual awakening, recovered life begins. The end of recovery is the beginning of intimacy. Looking closely at the literature of Alcoholics Anonymous, the mother-ship of all recovery programs, it becomes clear that this idea and the core of AA are entirely sympathetic. This is not a new idea, but what is new in our time is how recovery has become a life-style. We live in a day of talk show sycophants, shows whose ratings seem directly proportionate to the volume of confessional tears induced; of disgraced politicians, struggling to keep their jobs and who couldn't help it because the booze made them lie, cheat, and steal; and of the showy show of show business icons who've stopped puking in the potted palm and want the world to know "so, just maybe, Larry, I can be of some little help to just one someone else."

Recovery is *not* a lifestyle. Disease is *not* currency. Disease and recovery are not much of a basis of identity. "I'm Bill and I'm a recovering alcoholic" is a weak brew.

When an old friend had read an early draft of these words, he wrote to me, "I, myself, am a recovering Presbyterian, but I would rather tell you about the trapeze." Now, although I was once a Presbyterian as well and do not view Presbyterianism as a disease, I fully concur with what my friend was saying. What I hear in his statement is, "Get over it, cowboy, there's work to be done. Tell me your new story!"

In the March 20, 1995 issue of *The New Yorker*, Andrew and Thomas Delbanco asked the question: Is AA still OK? Although time, flux, and circumstances forced them to leave the answer open, I felt some uneasiness in myself, sensing the coming of a monotonous drone heard from church basements nationwide, a Western OM, pronounced "I'M," drowning out the time-faded laughter of men and women victorious, each in their own way but all by helping others, over the nastiness of alcoholism for just that one day. The Delbancos speak of the "incessant whine of the injured self" in Twelve Step meetings and the loss of the true meaning of the Twelfth Step, helping oneself by helping another. "It was the *disease* that did it" has replaced the notion of responsibility, and the intimacy of helping another is uprooted by the gruesome loneliness and slow soul murder of the ". . . but I'm OK" crowd.

I am not going to detour into the current fashion of decrying the victim culture. That is an endless political shuffle that leads nowhere. Yes, ours is a victim culture. No, we shouldn't pay attention. Yes, no, yes, no . . . while suffering continues all about us. The first of the Four Noble Truths of the Buddha is "Life suffers." There is deep suffering all around us, and I try, and often fail, to force myself to look at it without the darkened lenses of cynicism brought about so easily by the aberrations of the television culture and sponsored lives. I believe that those who have joined the "whine of the injured self" are truly injured in ways not at all clear to them, just as I was. In early recovery, I was desperate to understand how I had gotten into such a mess and was happy to hear that perhaps I really wasn't at fault. I learned, in time, that there is no fault in this business! There is only responsibility and that is mine and mine alone.

Recovery ends as we join wholeheartedly into a community and begin to see the whole of the past. As we get to know others in community, we glimpse reflections of ourselves until the day comes when we face ourselves directly. The story of the past is completed and flows seamlessly into the future. This is a time of reconciliation and self-acceptance. Don't hold back. It is vitally important to give up thinking of yourself as "always recovering, never recovered." Do you want "recovering alcoholic" to become your trump card, to be brought out when you don't see some other way to go? This is the "victim" trap. "I can't help it, I'm a recovering alcoholic" can become "I'm sorry. I didn't handle that well."

You can begin to see that the emphasis on recover*ing* is an emphasis on continuing addiction. Addiction to recovery is the subtlest trap, after which there aren't many left. Alcoholism is no longer the illness. Recovery is. And beneath the illness of recovery is the deepest illness of all: the illness of delusion. If you don't want to stay ill, then throw away your medicine when you see that it has become the illness. As you tell your story and listen to the stories of others, listen for your wholeness. It will arise if you watch for it. If we are "perfect and complete, exactly as we are, lacking nothing," as Daidoshi says, then why all this emphasis on mindfulness, storytelling and community? Mindfulness, storytelling, and community are where we realize our perfection; it's where the pepper goes in the soup. As you use the tools of Ordinary Recovery, you will arrive at the end of recovery. Please don't let the folks who insist on constant recovering deter you.

When they push too hard, refer them to the title page of the third edition of *Alcoholics Anonymous*, the "Big Book," published in 1976, where it says "The *Story* of How Many Thousands of Men and Women Have *Recovered* from Alcoholism"(emphasis added). Please watch your story carefully and stay awake to the present moment. You will recover. Pay attention here. *You will recover; but you will never be cured.*

Here is the story of how I became conscious of passing from "recovering" to "recovered." Your story will be different, but I hope you will see it as clearly as I saw mine.

I spent many of my young years and many additional summers on my mother's family farm deep in the rock-and-roll triangle of west Tennessee, forty-five miles from Memphis, closer yet to Jackson and Bolivar. My great-uncle Lacey, my maiden great-aunt Sadie, and their sister Sam, my grandmother, lived there in a home with white pillars and outdoor plumbing. In the summers, cicadas sang in the massive oaks and the world smelled like dust and honeysuckle. It was a big working farm—corn and cotton, milkcows, and walking horses. I spent hours every day alone, swinging on the tire swing in the front yard or wandering in the apple orchards. I built forts in the pasture next to the house. I chased the goats and dared to approach the cows. When I was five I had a pony named Dolly. Dolly got into the clover one night and died of it by the next afternoon.

From the time I was nine years old, I could ride horses on my own. My first was an old work horse named Whitey, as gentle a horse as there ever was. In the early summer mornings of 1951 and for many summers thereafter I would ride out to the fields beyond the barn, down toward an old home known as the Polk Place, which had belonged to a distant relative at the time of the Civil War. Along the way were open meadows broken by clumps of oak trees and by deep fissures in the earth, overgrown with ferns and littered with deadfall. The largest of these sinkholes once held the corpse of a goat that had been kicked to death by a mule and tossed there by one of the workers. I noted the progress of the corpse every morning that summer as the flesh rotted and the hide turned to tattered leather and then fell away until only the bones remained, ribs crushed, but otherwise the simulacrum of the living animal. I would look, from the edge of the arroyo, until Whitey grew impatient.

There were evil horseflies and clouds of gnats in those meadows and copses. I marveled as we rode at how Whitey could move his ears in great circles or lay them flat against his mane to combat these critters.

On hot afternoons, I would climb up into the hayloft of the main barn and try to smoke cornsilk in a corncob pipe. I'd drink a Royal Crown Cola (an RC, that is) or an Orange Crush and eat a moon pie—chocolate, marshmallow, and graham cracker—that satisfied like little else. Sometimes I put aspirin in the RC because I'd heard that would get you drunk, whatever drunk was. If it worked, it took a long time.

This was holy ground for me. It was a sacred place where I tasted honeysuckle and cool mint, and saw, in the normal course of the days, birth and violent death. I entered adolescence there, a dizzying passage into unsuspected desires and glorious release. I kissed a girl there for the first time. I read *Battle Cry* by Leon Uris, some pages over and over. "Their bodies melted together like butter," I think it said.

I can reclaim it all in a moment today just as it was—horseflies, dust, and gravel road to town—and still draw no conclusions about it. It didn't "mean" anything. Life doesn't "mean" when the marrow is touched. I lived those years too intimately to need to understand them. Dylan Thomas wrote ". . . I was green and carefree, famous among the barns/ About the happy yard and singing as the farm was home." His poem, "Fern Hill," is an ominous one. The years ahead would lose the gentle shine of those reckless Tennessee summers; "the farm forever fled," Thomas says later in the poem.

Years later, in the summer of 1994, I was walking slowly, very slowly, along a dirt path bordered by dusty grasses and small flowering plants. It was a hot day in August, over ninety-five degrees at noon and the air was still, carrying the varied sounds of three hundred other slow walkers; bare feet, boots, running shoes, the universal clogs, and Birkenstocks blending to a calming whisper of mindful movement. This was the practice of walking meditation at Plum Village, a Buddhist community in the Dordogne area of southwest France where I was spending the summer. I was at the very head of this procession, walking and holding the diminutive, powerful left hand of the Zen master Thich Nhat Hanh, known as Thây. More accurately, Thây's gentle left hand was guiding my right.

Shortly before, a friend and I had been standing near the bathrooms, waiting our turn and joking about the primitive plumbing, when he suddenly looked quite grave and said "It's Thây," darting his eyes to the right, behind me. I turned in time to see him walking toward me and as his eyes caught mine he held his hand out in invitation and smiled gently, nodding and pausing for only a moment. I took his hand, "engulfed it," as a monk told me later and joined in his unhurried pace. This walking meditation is an integral part of everyday life at Plum Village. The point is to walk, mindful of your feet on the earth, breathing in rhythm with your steps. Breathing in, I step on the beautiful earth. Breathing out, I know I am home. Step. Home. Step. Home.

On most days, Thây would ask two of the many children at Plum Village to walk with him. I am over six feet tall, weigh about 180 pounds, and that day was wearing a bright yellow T-shirt with baggy black cotton pants and rubber sandals. I was fifty-two years old. Not a child, and not likely to be mistaken for one. As we walked, I struggled to concentrate on the present moment, to feel the earth pushing against my rubber sandals. Here I was walking with a Zen master who had the universal respect of his peers, who had been nominated for the Nobel peace prize by Dr. Martin Luther King, Jr., who had founded the Buddhist Peace Fellowship, and who was the sole author of the radical idea of "engaged Buddhism." This is no ordinary teacher. He is a monk and lives like one.

I had been a practicing Zen Buddhist for about four years at this time. I sat in meditation twice a day, visited whenever possible the monastery in the Catskills where my teacher lived, and did my best to fulfill the rigorous requirements of lay practice. I was a beginner.

As I walked with Thây, I struggled to do it right—to stay in the moment, not to falter. This was final exams, first day on the job, and the final seconds of a tied game all at once. I drifted into it fairly easily. On only three occasions did I drift off entirely, including one time when my mind slipped all the way back to New Jersey and got into a heated discussion with my wife about what color to paint the shutters on our house. Each of the three times, I felt a gentle squeeze on my hand. The first two times, I simply returned to my breath and walked on. The third time, the time I was arguing with Pauline in New Jersey, when the pressure came, I laughed out loud. So did Thây. I glanced at him. He was smiling broadly and laughed again.

A few minutes later, we crossed a small stream, one before the other and with hands free, and entered a clearing deep in the trees. The air was cool and the stream splashed gently. While we waited for the others to arrive, I sat cross-legged on the damp ground. I lost myself there for a few moments and when I looked up, my old horse Whitey was standing by the stream, composed entirely of soft light and dust motes. His hooves were muddy. He stood by the stream where we had found a huge snapping turtle, shot by a rifle through the shell, just the day before. The sun slanted through

Tennessee skies and slender saplings. I was as surely back home as if I had never left.

The moment passed quickly. The ancient ground of the Dordogne was once again beneath me. Whitey returned to the Tennessee earth. Thich Nhat Hanh was sitting next to me, solid in his brown robes.

If I had to say that there was a moment when my recovery ended, then that was it. I had come full circle to awe and wonder. I was connected to earth, memory, self, and other. The barriers constructed by thirty years of addiction were broken and I was whole again. It had happened as such things always do: very gradually, unnoticed, so gently and all at once.

The catastrophe of active addiction had been transformed. I still go to AA meetings and suspect that I always will. I know that I am a recovered alcoholic, and I go there for the gifts of community and the transitional stories I continue to hear. When you are recovered you will know, bone deep, that there is nothing that your addiction did to you that could be undone, that has not been undone. Ordinary life awaits. The tools are the same. The problems are the same. You are transformed. Many people have had this experience. There are two truths about it. One: You can't fake it. Two: You can't deny it.

Now, life happens. Pay attention.

BREATHING ROOM

An old Zen saying cautions us not to mistake a fish's eye for a pearl. If you think you've seen the light, check it out with someone who knows where the switches are.

Rage at the Short Hills Mall

T HE SHORT HILLS MALL in Short Hills, New Jersey is a labyrinth of trendy and established shops. Gucci is there with its bridle bit shoes for the unhorsed and Tiffany's has hold of an important corner. There is a bookstore, a candy store, two theme restaurants (fifties joint and New York grill), a Neiman Marcus, and a Saks. All the franchise shops are there, selling cookies and luggage and more. The chain stores born of the seventies are there as well, selling adventure to the housebound (banana's republicans) and erotica to the power bound (Victorian secrets leer through lace and push-tittie bras). If you want to look like you were born with money, live on a ranch, and wear only humble old worn-out clothes, Ralph'll help in an instant. Or you can go get maced with Bloomingdale fragrance if you fear you smell too real.

The Short Hills Mall is quite a spot. Hyperbole and metaphor are right at home here. Just for starters, the place provides an infinitely repeatable rite of adult affirmation: You go there; you look around; you buy. You have succeeded.

"I went to Short Hills and found something I wanted," you say. Then, "I hate that mall." Here is your greater success. "I have braved the jungle," is your message. "Against My Will but for the Greater Good, and I prevailed." The triumphant statement is inevitably followed by a knowing shake of the head and a rueful smile. Later, you go back. You have faith, church, and liturgy.

I am a suburb-dwelling, married white male, over fifty. The mall, I'm told, is my new community center, my town square, and village green. It is not! It is a place to go and buy stuff. I do that and when I leave I feel, at least, off center. In the years that I have been free of substance addiction, I have grown more sensitive to these environments, not less. I look forward to the day that I will go shopping with only a shopping list and a sense of equanimity. Now, I fear, I go with an attitude. I feel superior to the folks there, all the while suffering and denying it. I am feeling the suffering of no light, no air, no comfort. I am feeling in myself the suffering of addictive buying and the suffering of avoiding addictive buying. I become entranced in that place and the soul suffers. In that place I am out of my mind. I am dis-incarnate.

There is one shopping trip at the Short Hills Mall that stands out in my mind. It was the holiday season of 1995 and I joined hundreds of others in the annual exercise in giving and getting. I drank black coffee from a coffee theme place and then ate a cookie from Mrs. Fields. Coffee, sugar, chocolate! I was stimulated and no longer averse. These were *my* people now! I achieved a version of power-laced serenity available only in a place where the light and air are poisoned and where there is a beckoning tendril of eroticism edging from every object offered for sale.

This does not seem a likely stage for transformation, particularly at holiday time, when the whole crowd of people was supercharged on anger, greed, eros, and hustle. There was a crackle in the air like ozone on fire. It felt like the Davidson County fair in Nashville in 1959. Color, movement, noise, and scent all wrapped up in an amorphous and mysterious energy that hummed just outside the fragile skin.

I rushed from store to store, buying heedlessly. The Nature Company, yes, a field guide for each kid; spiders, lizards, stars, trees, fancy soaps at this place, simple clothes at that one; science fiction, computer books, fairy tales, and Buddha stories at the bookshop. Candles for the zendo; scented oils for the living room.

I consume, therefore I am. By the time I left I was drunk with greed and rage. As I was pulling into the traffic flow, a skim latte grasped between my thighs and another brownie resting on the seat, a fellow in a shining black 4WD vehicle that could handle the Serengeti with ease cut me off. The driver, predictably a middle-aged man in a suit and tie, gave me the finger, laughed, and roared off down the ramp, in pursuit of better lions to kill, I guess. I did not take this well. Mick Jagger was singing, "It's just that evil life that's got me in its sway," and I was swinging to some ancient rhythms and it was dark outside. Wolf brain was unleashed and I was going to kill that son-of-a-bitch in his god-forsaken land-raping status symbol. I took after him; which was no mean feat in that traffic and on a circular down ramp wide enough for only one car. My tires squealed and my brakes stunk. I spilled hot coffee on my dick. Nowhere is my darker character better revealed than behind the wheel of my car.

I never caught him.

Two years and a few months prior to this frenzy I had received the Five Noble Precepts of Buddhism from Thich Nhat Hanh. I offer them to you in their entirety. Although these precepts have their roots in the very beginning of Buddhism, Thich Nhat Hanh has thoughtfully brought them very much up to date. Some of what you are about to read will probably confound you. There is no ancient dogma here.

The First Precept

Aware of the suffering caused by the destruction of life, I vow to cultivate compassion and learn ways to protect the lives of people, animals, plants and minerals. I am determined not to kill, not to let others kill, and not to condone any act of killing in the world, in my thinking, and in my way of life.

The Second Precept

Aware of the suffering caused by exploitation, social injustice, stealing, and oppression, I vow to cultivate loving kindness and learn ways to work for the well-being of people, animals, plants, and minerals. I vow to practice generosity by sharing my time, energy, and material resources with those who are in real need. I am determined not to steal and not to possess anything that should belong to others. I will respect the property of others, but I will prevent others from profiting from human suffering or the suffering of other species on Earth.

The Third Precept

Aware of the suffering caused by sexual misconduct, I vow to cultivate responsibility and learn ways to protect the safety and integrity of individuals, couples, family, and society. I am determined not to engage in sexual relations without love and a long-term commitment. To preserve the happiness of myself and others, I am determined to respect my commitments and the commitments of others. I will do everything in my power to protect children from sexual abuse and to prevent couples and families from being broken by sexual misconduct.

The Fourth Precept

Aware of the suffering caused by unmindful speech and the inability to listen to others, I vow to cultivate loving speech and deep listening in order to bring joy and happiness to others and relieve others of their suffering. Knowing that words can create happiness or suffering, I vow to learn to speak truthfully, with words that inspire self-confidence, joy, and hope. I am determined not to spread news that I do not know to be certain and not to criticize or condemn things of which I am not sure. I will refrain from uttering words that can cause division or discord, or that can cause the family or the community to break. I will make all efforts to reconcile and resolve all conflicts, however small.

The Fifth Precept

Aware of the suffering caused by unmindful consumption, I vow to cultivate good health, both physical and mental, for myself, my family, and my society by practicing mindful eating, drinking, and consuming. I vow to ingest only items that preserve peace, well-being, and joy in my body, in my consciousness, and in the collective body and consciousness of my family and society. I am determined not to use alcohol or any other intoxicant or to ingest foods or other items that contain toxins, such as certain TV programs, magazines, books, films, or conversations. I am aware that to damage my body or my consciousness with these poisons is to betray my ancestors, my parents, my society, and future generations. I will work to transform violence, fear, and confusion in myself and in society by practicing a diet for myself and for society. I understand that a proper diet is crucial for self-transformation and for the transformation of society.

My understanding of these precepts today is that by transforming myself I am transforming society. As a person who was given the gift of even modest insight into the reality of transcendent self, it is my uninvited obligation to see such darkness as it is. There is no virtue in this, only necessity. If I continue to dance with the three poisons, I am at risk of a hellish narcotic rapture—if not booze, then mere insensibility and a waste of the gift I was given. On that day in the Short Hills Mall, I had fallen far away from the understanding and practice of these vows. Rather than transforming myself, I was cooperating with the dominant culture, which can destroy me. Rather than transforming society, I was enlivening it while dancing with Thanatos.

The Five Noble Precepts are the antidote. Please read them carefully. They describe a life of service and responsibility. It is a life envisioned in Step Eight of AA, "the end of isolation from man and god."

In AA we say that we strive for spiritual progress rather than for spiritual perfection. A Buddhist teacher says we are all perfect and complete, lacking nothing. When questioned, he says. "I have nothing to teach you." When pressed further, he says, "You already have the answer. Your task is to realize it, to actualize it." Alcoholics Anonymous is uniquely American and, as such, uniquely pragmatic. The statement about progress rather than perfection is a pragmatic and very wise one, based on the assumption that the ideal of perfection is a dangerous one for any addict. Some argue that perfectionism is the background against which most addictions are played out. For me, alcohol and drugs gave the illusion of control. While operating in that illusion, my life was perfect. When the illusion cracked, as it always did when the substance faded, I was left in imperfection and fear, both totally soluble in Glenfiddich or Gallo.

I understand the Buddhist point of view differently, however, and that is the difference that made the difference. I do strive for perfection, without the superstitious fear that the striving itself will lead to the barroom or the dealers' street corner. The wino's curse is "If something good happens, it will end if you talk about it." A corollary to the wino's curse is, "If you hope for the best, you'll never get it." I endeavor to use the Five Noble Precepts like a compass set on the North Star. I remain on my journey, certain that it will end where it should and that that end will not be the North Star. And it won't be the Short Hills Mall either. The precepts help me, however falteringly, to live in the world of nurturance rather than the pervasive and dominant world of exploitation.

That evening of rage at the Short Hills Mall was a great teacher. Here was another sacred catastrophe offering hope and change. That anonymous fellow was my Land Rover Boddhisattva. I came unglued at his gesture and his laugh. They drove me back to the Five Noble Precepts and ahead to a deeper commitment to Buddhist practice.

How to Build a Cathedral

~~~~~~~~~~~~~~~~~~~~~~~

A NUMBER OF YEARS AGO, I was talking with a group of friends who shared a common desire to stay out of trouble with alcohol and drugs. I was having a pretty hard time of it. I had been fired six months earlier from a job as an editor and had been working as a typist, a file clerk, and a day laborer to keep a few bucks in my pocket. I was three months behind on my rent on my east side two-room apartment and threatened with eviction. My girlfriend and I had broken up, again, and I was hurt, again. I was stretched thin. I am sure that as I sat and talked about this I sounded like I felt—frightened, angry, and without resources. This is a dangerous spot for someone so accustomed to the instant nirvana of a couple of shots of gin. No ongoing work, no stable place to live, and romantically obsessed—an unstable position for someone who has thrown away his crutches.

There was a fellow there that day I hadn't seen before—lanky, hirsute, and dressed all in black. He told the group that "what Bill needs" was what he, Johnny Cash we'll call him, had. What Johnny had was a house in Woodstock built on the side of a hill. The hill was all his property and, he told us, he had planted a small tree on top of that hill where he would go every weekend morning to sit and meditate for a few minutes. What Bill needed, then, was a house on a hill in Woodstock, a tree, and a shovel. What Bill had was about two hundred dollars and a pending court date. My feelings about

his unsolicited advice were not charitable. They still aren't. I was furious. In that type of meeting, cross talk is prohibited so, thankfully, I didn't have the opportunity to tell this fellow what I was thinking. There was an ugly silence in the room. He had crossed a line by giving advice and in the process had let us know facts that were irrelevant. After a moment or two, a friend of mine who lived up in Spanish Harlem got his hand up. Let's call him the bathroom Bodhisattva. He shared, in words other than those I'll use here, that, as far as he was concerned, if he couldn't meditate while hiding in the bathroom, he wouldn't be able to meditate on the top of (it was here that his language got real colorful) a mountain in Woodstock. He went on to say that he meditated every day in the bathroom because he lived with his large family, parents and siblings, and that was the only private place in a very small apartment.

Henry Miller said, "If there is to be any peace it will come through being, not having." The bathroom Bodhisattva showed me that, and, to be fair, Johnny Cash pointed the way. It was on that day that I began to understand the great value of a private place, a cathedral of one's own for stillness and silence.

Properly a cathedral is the place of a bishop's throne, the diocesan home. I don't want to stretch that metaphor, but I don't want to give up the word. To me, a cathedral is a place of quiet and transcendent majesty. Like the Cathedral of St. John the Divine in New York, where my wife and I were married and where our son was baptized, a cathedral of one's own is a place of personal communion with the power of things as they are. Within the cathedral are relics of the past and reminders of one's greater self. There is quiet, there is beauty, and there is the reality of focused intention and purpose.

My first cathedral centered around a small table I found on the street, cleaned up, and put in a corner of my tiny apartment. I bought a little wooden box in a neighborhood thrift shop for just a dollar or two. The box has a gold inlay of a windswept tree against its black wood. It's about the size of a Walkman radio. I put a cheap ceramic incense burner on the table and an old piece of silk cloth, cream colored with circles of cerulean blue edged with earthy brown. I would sit by that table every morning and read Thomas Merton, drinking black coffee and smoking one cigarette after another. I wrote out a prayer of Merton's, and put it in a dimestore frame. Here is that prayer:

> My Lord God, I have no idea where I am going. I do not
> see the road ahead of me. I cannot know for certain
> where it will end. Nor do I really know myself, and the

fact that I think I am following your will does not mean that I am actually doing so. But I believe that the desire to please you does in fact please you. And I hope that I will never do anything apart from that desire. And I know that if I do this you will lead me by the right road, though I may know nothing about it. Therefore I will trust you always though I may seem to be lost and in the shadow of death. I will not fear, for you are ever with me, and you will never leave me to face my perils alone.

When you build your cathedral, make it entirely your own. A candle provides a pleasant light and an opportunity to develop ritual. As you light your candle, you might say a prayer for all those you love. "Lighting this candle, I offer its warmth and light to all those I have known and lost, to all those I know today, and to all those I have yet to meet. I vow to keep an open place in my heart for the unknown one who awaits." If you light incense from the candle, you can watch the tendrils of smoke as they drift and disappear and use that moment to return to your center. Lighting the incense can accompany lighting the candle and you can join the two into a longer ceremony of gratitude. Let your heart rise with the smoke and bless the universe it inhabits.

It is a comforting practice to place family pictures in your cathedral. If that is not possible for you, then find pictures of loved ones or of those you don't know who have touched you. Don't fear that you are practicing idolatry by placing a picture of the Buddha or of Jesus there. For a long time I kept a picture of my daughter at age one beside a picture of myself at the same age. These pictures remind us of the ancestors and of those others to whom we are responsible. The ancestors move ahead, calling us to follow, while the living support us as we support them. When you are in the presence of these pictures, you can look at them deeply and express your gratitude to those who have gone before and to those who are with you now.

I have a bill of sale for a human being that sits in a place of prominence among the pictures of my family and other teachers. This document was signed by a relative of mine in the dark days before the Civil War. The man who was sold was named Jim and he is as surely an ancestor of mine as the unwitting blood relative whose cramped signature diminished his own humanity. They both remind me of who I could be.

The altar is the vital center of the cathedral; from it is illuminated the transformation we long for. I used to live in a township that seemed the epicenter of materialism and greed to me. Although there were no consciously constructed altars within most of the homes there, what was worshipped was clear. You needed to spend only a few minutes in such a home to find its center. You have seen these homes. The people who live in them are for the most part good-hearted, but there is no deliberate center to their homes. This is the curse of affluence: more and more and more flows in while nothing flows out. We all have our liturgy, our altars, and our creed. We need to learn to see them and, if they are dark, bring light to them. What pictures do you have on your walls? What is the center of attention in any room? While you are constructing the altar for your cathedral, consider where you are placing it.

Some of the homes in that town were filled with fresh flowers year round. This was about money, not humility in the face of beauty. Anyone can buy flowers or have them bought, but such conspicuous displays are about the buyer, not the flowers. As your dwelling is transformed into a cathedral, you may wish to place fresh flowers or greenery in special places. Pick them yourself; choose them carefully and be prudent. Perhaps only one flower or one pine spray is all you need. Promise yourself that before their freshness is gone, you will pass them on to someone else. Practice abundance, not affluence. In abundance we give away because there is nothing extra; in affluence we hold tight because we're afraid of never having enough. In abundance we are healed while healing; in affluence we sicken and die standing up and talking.

When you place your flowers, you may wish to breathe in and out while you compose a prayer of mindfulness that they inspire. "Placing this beautiful flower in my home, I am aware of the serenity it offers and I vow to carry that serenity into my day and to share it with all I meet."

In transforming your dwelling into a cathedral, choose every action carefully. Be mindful of this sacred place where you take refuge. Create prayers as you transform this place. "As I see the transformation of my home from the mundane to the sacred, I vow to dwell mindfully in its very ordinariness and to carry what I make here into the marketplace."

Consider your entire home your cathedral and watch as it grows. Make it your own and share it. Until recently, my family spent a month or two each summer in an old house on Lake Champlain in upper New York State. We last had the place in the summer of 1996 and many guests during the weeks we were there. Among them were John and David and Emily Sell. They stayed in a separate cabin, but we spent many hours together, day and night. On the last night of their stay, we all had dinner together. The house had become a cathedral over the previous few years. There was nothing special about it to the unknowing eye, but to my family it was as rich a place as the Cathedral of St. John the Divine. There was a small statue of the Medicine Buddha on an old table by the front door. There was a small earthen bowl that my wife had made, filled with fireplace ash and incense dust. The furniture was old, not antique or precious, just old and loved. This is the house that the Sells walked into that night. Emily is my editor and I have known her for more years than either of us might wish to admit. She is a gracious person, and John, her husband, is a gifted man in many ways. He and I had climbed Hurricane Mountain just a few days before. He embarrassed me with his strength and endurance. On the way down, he practically ran. Their son David is an inquisitive and thoughtful child a couple of years older than my son.

Dinner stretched and stretched. The spaghetti and salad were consumed slowly and the chocolate ice cream with chocolate syrup was savored. Not one of the adults made a move to leave the table. We sat and talked until past eleven, telling stories and laughing at our follies and feeling good about our accomplishments. Our Cathedral on Lake Champlain rang with the communion of story and open caring. When the Sells were ready to leave, I said that their presence had blessed the place and that evenings like this were what I had longed for and had missed for many years. When I told them of my longing for more nights such as this, Emily just said "Me, too." John nodded his assent.

Here is what I offer to you. Get to work on your cathedral. It will never be finished, but the work glorifies the place. As the work continues, invite your friends over. Allow them to bless it and ask them to keep coming back. Your stories will grow and heal in this sacred place.

BREATHING ROOM

What do you have in your pockets? Is there anything there that is superfluous?

Find some small thing, a stone perhaps, and spend some time with it. Where was it before it was where you found it? What did it look like before it looks like it does now?

After you have considered these questions, put this thing in your pocket. Is there anything superfluous in your pocket now?

Rapture

~~~~~~~~~~~~~~~~~~~~~~~~~

THE REALM OF THE HUNGRY GHOST

MY DAUGHTER HAS CHOSEN a simple life for herself. It is no small thing that she is able to do this. She works for a government agency and lives in a major metropolitan area. She is of an age to accumulate and complicate. She chooses not to. When I am with her I feel overly complicated and overwhelmed with stuff. The feeling doesn't usually last. My life cannot be as simple as hers because the circumstances are so different. She is single; I have four children at home. There are other differences: age, passions, energy. My life is as simple as I can make it today and I continue to try to simplify it further. My daughter is one of my best teachers in this endeavor. When I asked her what her spiritual practice was, she replied without hesitation, "Running." She has run in the Boston Marathon three times and is on a quest to run one marathon in each of the fifty states. She has also competed in a number of triathlons. Like so many people who have seen darker days, she moves lightly and easily on the earth. The AA phrase is that she "wears her life like a loose garment." She does, often effortlessly, what I sometimes struggle to do.

One vow of the Tiep Hien Order is "to live simply and sanely, content with just a few possessions." In the early fall of 1996, I went through a period of Porsche frenzy. What I wanted was a Carrera Cabriolet, silver and fully equipped. I went to showrooms. I bought *Car and Driver*, a real anomaly in my magazine rack, which runs more to *Tricycle, New Age, Outside, Men's Health, Mountain Bike, Shambhala Sun,* and— OK—*Vanity Fair* and *GQ*. I looked up Porsche sites on the Internet and pointed out the sleek little devils to whatever member of the family happened to be with me when I saw one. I was possessed. Hungry. In the morning when I refreshed my vows, the vow to live simply would stick in my throat. My years of active addiction, demanding as they did that I refine the art of rationalization and justification, served me well. In those years I could get away with the most aberrant nonsense. I fooled a lot of people, but no one more than myself. One of the most evil deceits was the belief that I was getting over, when in fact I was as transparent as an eleven-year-old.

This Porsche mania went on and on. My rationalization, the clever cover-up, was that this was a "classic," a collector's item that I would pass on to my children. Another rationalization was that for the first time in my life I could afford such a car. (I couldn't.) There was the "I deserve it" rationalization and the "appreciation of fine art" one. There was the one about the "sheer sensual pleasure of driving a finely made machine," and I even spent a little time trying to convince myself that owning a Porsche was a clever way to hide assets. Infinitely clever I was, but always there was this wee doubt. That damned vow wouldn't let loose of me. It didn't so much cause guilt as it pointed to my deeper nature. Like my daughter, like my wife, like most of us, living simply and sanely is what is most deeply felt. And like many of us, but unlike my daughter and my wife, I am not inclined to follow such sensible, spiritual urges when the *need* has gotten hold and is driving me.

The hungry ghost is never satisfied. That is his nature. In Buddhism, the hungry ghost is a creature with a vast and empty body, and a tiny throat. He is always hungry and never satisfied. In the hungry ghost realm, you are with the enraptured, in the words of Chögyam Trungpa, "by the process of expanding, becoming rich, *consuming!*" (Emphasis added.) We insist on more. This is the nation of the biggest, the newest, and the best; and in the process we eat up the earth's resources at a discouraging rate and, just as dangerous, we lead lives of rationalization and rapture.

Putting down the drug or putting the cork in the bottle is only the beginning of sobriety. Bill Wilson said of AA, "We operate a spiritual kindergarten." Best-selling books to the contrary, I did not learn everything I need to know in kindergarten. When the booze disappears, another substance will appear to sustain the rapture. If substances fail, behaviors will surface. Absent behaviors, compulsive thought patterns will arise; one can drown in one's own self-importance. Attachment to anything seems preferable to an ongoing process of letting go. The poet told us what freedom was: nothing left to lose. He didn't tell us how to get there. Beyond the big thirsts, the rag-a-tag minutiae have their pull as well. If I can't be obsessed with gin or with God, then consumer goods will do. Which brings me back to that Porsche Turbo Carrera.

I was going on about that car at dinner one night. A silver one or black? John, my snowboarding fourteen-year-old stepson, was listening thoughtfully. John is no stranger to desire. He looks less like a person and more like a pile of clothes when he is sitting down. His sunglasses are molded to his face and his patois is nearly indecipherable. In this instance, however, his words were clear. "Bill," he said, "if you buy a Porsche, the very first morning you wake up and see it out in the driveway, you'll wonder why you ever bought it. You'll be ashamed of yourself."

Thus ended Porsche mania. John had told me the truth. The rapture of consuming was so powerful, its ecstatic swirl so hypnotic, that I had forgotten who I was. John remembered. The hungry ghost lost that round, but he's as persistent as booze ads and my dark twin loves him madly.

I would like a Ford F-150 Flareside, but that's another story.

God's Will

~~~~~~

I N T H E S U M M E R O F 1 9 9 1 , I attended the Advanced
School for Addiction Studies at Rutgers University. I was
one of the few students there who did not work "in the
field"; that is, although I was a qualified addictions counselor,
I did not work as one. For two weeks I was surrounded by
well-meaning people, almost all of them recovered or recovering addicts and alcoholics. There was a very vocal, generally
young, minority who insisted, with one voice and loudly, that
they had been chosen by God not to die from their addictions.
One fellow in particular told an assembly of several hundred,
during an outdoor AA meeting on a beautiful and sunny day,
that he was one of "the chosen people."

I do not believe this. I believe as well that such an idea is
dangerous to the addict and to the larger world. I reject the
idea of chosen people; our human history, at play in the
world, is too rich for such arrogance. Our mutual heritage is
thinned by the presumption of superiority, based, as it is,
solely on superstition. By superstition I mean a murky understanding of cause and effect. I can believe, if I wish, that I
was saved from death by alcohol by some power greater than
myself. In fact, I have such a belief. It does not follow that I
was somehow chosen as especially worthy of saving, worthier
than others. I believe that my sobriety is a matter of what
Buddhists call karma. I believe, that is, that the sum of all my
thoughts and actions brought me to that stunning moment of

realization, my own subdued white light, when I saw clearly that I did not have to drink. The veil of addiction was lifted, just for a moment, when I happened to be looking. I also believe that I did not have to follow that light; karma is not determinism or my old Presbyterian superstition of predestination. I merely saw an option, with my heart, and chose it. My sobriety was the flower that, growing in the darkness for over forty years, suddenly bloomed, all of a sudden, in a breakthrough that has forever altered the course of my life. Often one hears that the alcoholic or addict does not come to recovery "on the wings of victory." I disagree. We come to recovery on just those wings. We are, for a moment, victorious over thirst, fear, and ignorance. That awakening is not an event. It is an opportunity. Rather than determinism or being chosen by a capricious God who has, by extension, killed a number of my relatives and friends, I see the moment of realization as the result of karma and the continuity of sobriety as the ongoing results of that moment.

In each moment, we plant new seeds of karma in the old ones. Infinite change is possible through the simple desire to change. As in Thomas Merton's prayer (see pages 72–73), "I believe that the desire to please you does in fact please you."

The breakthrough of realizing that we do not have to drink—solving that koan, severing that knot—plants the seed for every positive moment to follow. This is deutero-learning, learning about learning, and, followed assiduously, will lead inevitably to a life of joy, service, and genuine sobriety. It is not the end of addiction. It is the end of ignorance about addiction. Awakened, we are free to act "virtuously" in order to stay awake. It is an easy matter to continue to sleep. There are ample addictions to keep us snoozing for a lifetime. It is, however, an easier matter, through practice, to recognize the addictions and to wear them down. That flower, long in darkness, blooms better in the light and spreads its seeds in a wider arc. The seed planted at the moment of awakening can be watered eternally.

Individual karma, in the Hindu understanding, is infinitely variable according to choices made, which must include choices made in opposition to karma! Karma provides the situation, not the actions in the situation. This free will or freedom of choice is made possible by the reality of the freedom of inner consciousness or *atman*. In Buddhist understanding, however, *atman*, or in the West, *soul*, is denied. There is *no* independently existing self, soul, or spirit. As Thich Nhat Hanh puts it, an apple is made up of many non-apple elements. I have had the personal experience of the "falling away of body and mind" and know intimately the reality of no-separation. I have walked on the grounds around my home in blissful connection with the pin oaks and Japanese maples. I know and celebrate the truth of compassion, of mutual suffering and a desire to relieve it. When I said to Lyn Fine, a treasured friend and a dharma teacher in the Tiep Hien Order, "Hey, you're the teacher, not me," she gently set me straight, saying, "No distinctions my friend. You're the teacher too."

In the world of this and that, I choose to see within myself a separate spark that I tend and that is tended by "the ten thousand things," as Buddhists refer to the whole phenomenal universe. I may not have a separate being, but if I carry my particular faulty liver into a bar, I am in awful trouble. Drinking with the ten thousand things will get *me* drunk. I'll go back to the hospital while the ten thousand things crawl under the covers for the night. That liver, along with the havoc it can create, is unique, and in the greater community I can pay attention to it.

A reprise: When the veil of addiction is lifted, that is not the end of addiction. It is merely the end of delusion. It is the beginning of awareness of addiction. Addictions are endless. Addiction to recovery is one. The process after awakening is about staying awake, a constant round of letting go.

The Twelve Steps have an astuteness that makes it perilous to ignore them. There is a purity in the ideas of cleaning house, paying attention to the mind, and helping others that has made AA the most successful abstinence program ever. How, then, are you supposed to proceed, believing that the Twelve Steps contain the promise of freedom, but without the anchor of a belief in a God who's running the show, a benevolent God of rules and judgment?

I answer that question in many ways, and all those answers add up to one simple one: you do it by doing it. Action precedes understanding. I was driven by devils. I ran from my suffering on the only path I could see.

Since I believe that my recovery was more likely a matter of karma than of intervention by a capricious God, I found myself challenged by the other desirable "steps" that are necessary to maintain freedom from alcohol. Particularly nagging was the idea of meditating and praying to increase my "knowledge of God's will" for me. The answer came, once more in the understanding of karma. Past karma is just that—past. I cannot undo the past, although I can undo my shame-based attachment to it. The karma of the eternal present, however, is subject to my desire and action. Although I may know nothing of what "God's will" *should* mean, I can choose to say that it is *to be kind*. In the excellent book *Violence and*

Compassion by His Holiness the Dalai Lama and Jean-Claude Carriere, I learned to my delight that the short read on Buddhism is that "It's better to be nice than to be nasty." To be nice, to be kind to your neighbor—that is God's will.

. . . And the Power to Carry That Out

~~~~~~

ALCOHOL IS A DEMANDING AND PERSISTENT PARTNER. My dark twin led me to mean compromises that became meaner and more exhausting as the years went by. In a vicious twist on the Zen archers paradox of "it" loosing the arrow, as archer and target disappear, there came a time when "it" walked, "it" drank, "it"—the dark twin—planned, schemed, loved, and worked.

I had an office in an old Victorian building on Lombard Street in San Francisco in those days, the late 1970s. I had abandoned my car after driving it under a truck, drunk, with no registration, insurance, or driver's license, so I would walk to and from Lombard Street and my home on California Street. To do so meant crossing Union Street, the home of my favorite watering hole, which I shall leave unnamed out of affection for the owner. "I" would intend to walk on, straight up Octavia to home; "it" would walk down Union to the bar. "It" would order a vodka while "I" swore I would drink only coffee. "It" would order more after "I" promised only one. I can feel to this day the incredulity I felt then of once more drinking for several hours and then heading to the liquor store for a gallon of wine to take home. "I" watched mesmerized as "it" prevailed. Again and again, day to day for over a year, "it" prevailed. I was possessed by a phantom of inconceivable power. It has never entirely left me. I contain an immortal karmic seed, waiting as patiently to bloom as the centennial plant.

The dark hound will never lose my scent. During those long years of drunken isolation, I developed "habit energy" that became my code. If you think you do not have a code to live by, understand that that is your code to live by. My code was written by that Cimmerian phantom, the "it" whose favorite potion was "V and V," vodka and valium. This was a code of sadness and evasion. It would be dishonest to be extravagant in describing it. I was not honest, but I knew what honesty was. I was loyal, but often to the wrong people. I was no more consistently Mr. Hyde than I was Dr. Jekyll. I was, most often, a dim mix of both, with a surplus of Hyde.

When I stopped drinking, I still had the same code. It was formed by habits built on the need to drink! In Buddhist psychology, my code would be said to be formed by habit energy.

In the previous chapter, I shared my understanding of "God's will" as it is prescribed in the eleventh of AA's Twelve Steps. The short form of my understanding is that God's will is unknowable and that it is the desire to do that will that is, itself, the totality of our achievement. As a Buddhist, I believe that through practice of the Eightfold Path, I am practicing God's will. I aspire daily to practice intelligently, with honesty, openness, and willingness. I aspire to be kind. I fail far more often than I succeed. I hope, nonetheless, never to lose that aspiration.

The final part of Step Eleven speaks of "the power to carry it [God's will] out." I believe that the persistence required to maintain my sobriety is resolutely joined to my

practice of "God's will." If I am to stay sober, I must move
from great thirst to great compassion. It is my belief that the
power that drives that movement is, in Sanskrit, *maitri-karuna,*
translated as kindness and compassion. The power to carry
out "God's will" or the divine purpose—to a Buddhist, enlightenment for all beings—is found in *maitri-karuna:* love.
Ironically, I am writing these words on Valentine's Day, the
one day of the year that gives love a bad name. I remember
another Valentine's Day not too many years ago when I saw
my daughter in New York for the first time in over sixteen
years. It was anger that drove us apart and it was love that
brought us together. Love, as I am using it here, is nonjudgmental caring. That kind of love grows only through develop-
ing the ability to listen and to understand deeply.

Let me relate a story a friend told me about love, although I'll change some of the identifying details. My friend
Dan was in Seattle a number of years back. He had gone to
an AA meeting there and a notorious longtime drunk who,
like many (like you maybe, like me in the early 1980s), attended meetings drunk, hit on him after the meeting. It was
winter time, cold and wet and blowy. After the meeting Dan
and the drunk walked the streets for a while, Dan talking the
AA line and the drunk listening as best he could. They ended
up in an alley beside a seafood restaurant. It was late at night
and Dan knew that his brand of AA was probably disappearing
into an ethanol fog and he knew as well that his compatriot
was listening and waiting to hit on him for a few bucks for a
local flophouse. When the time came, when it was too wet
and too cold for the poor drunk to hold off any longer, he
asked for the money. Dan told him no. "I don't have the
money for something like that, but you can stay out of the

cold and wet in here," he said, opening the top of the restaurant's trash dumpster. We can only imagine what it must have
smelled like. Dan held the top up while the man crawled in,
not knowing he had already had his last drink. This was his
final desolation—the sacred misery that opened his heart by
breaking it. I say that what my friend did was an act of intu-
itive loving. He would not do the violence of paying for yet
another night in a skidrow flophouse. He had listened and he
had understood and then he had acted with nonjudgmental
caring.

Blood in the Steel

~~~~~~~~~~~~~~~~~~~~~~~~~~~

I AM A MEMBER OF the Order of Interbeing, a Vietnamese Zen Buddhist community founded by the Zen master Thich Nhat Hanh. When I first heard the word Interbeing, long before I joined the order, I was puzzled and more than just a little distressed by it. It seemed so syntactically naive. Surely, I felt, this wonderful monk could have come up with a less ingenuous term.

I had been done in by my sophistication. Over time I have come to appreciate the clarity and courage in this simple construction. It *is* naive and, as such, it demands attention. And it is clear. All things "inter-are." Without the rainstorms, I would not have had my grapefruit juice this morning. Without the sawmill, you would not be reading these words. Lacey McDaniel is my ancestor in hard-scrabble west Tennessee farmland and so is the Indian sage, Shakyamuni Buddha. Without them, I would not be. We are co-dependent, a proscribed phrase in Twelve Step programs and one I would like to see cleared of such mean stigma. Nothing can exist alone, by itself. I am co-dependent with you at this very moment. We inter-are. Randomly I can express gratitude to my ancestors Howard Thurman, Friederich Nietzsche, Kuan Yin, and the enormous oak tree by the pond on Lacey Road near Medon, Tennessee. The rasp and rattle of sawgrass in the Mekong delta floats on the morning wind in Long Valley, New Jersey.

Walt Whitman wrote:

I find I incorporate gneiss, coal, long-threaded moss, fruits,
grains, esculent roots,
And am stucco'd with quadrupeds and birds all over.

Thich Nhat Hanh has explained the central Buddhist idea of emptiness by saying that each of us contains a lot of non-me elements. I am made up of the blood of the ancestors, the ancient rains of the primeval forests, and the rhythms of the sea just as a morning newspaper contains a lot of non-newspaper elements. Without the forest, the rain, the sun, the tree cutters, the wood, and metal elements of the saw, the silver and mercury of the printing, there would be no *Commercial Appeal* on doorsteps in Memphis.

We inter-are.

I live at the end of a quarter-mile long road, deep in the woodlands of northern New Jersey. My house is hunkered down on the side of a worn-down mountain and in the middle of twenty acres of forest land that I have left entirely alone. When I go for walking meditation, I rustle through leaves and grasses and pass by dense groves of trees. Birds cry and I often see deer, frozen in their watching me. There are coyotes here although I have never seen one. At night, the stars seem less than a mile away.

When I first stopped drinking, however, I lived in Manhattan. No deer there, and looking underfoot was more often a matter of hygiene than of aesthetics. The sensual was corrupted. I was surrounded by concrete and steel and the decibel level was just short of painful at most every hour. This was a long way from Medon, Tennessee. I began reading about mindfulness then and it seemed that what little there was on the subject was more likely to be centered in places like my present home than in the caverns of the city I made my way through every day. How was I supposed to be *with* the earth when I was stepping in chewing gum and dog crap? How was I to be mindful of the present moment when all I could hear were garbage trucks and taxi horns? How was I to pray my gratitude into the infinite with sirens going off and car alarms bleating for hours on end only yards away? Mindfulness was for those in the southwest of France, surrounded by vineyards and fields of sunflowers, not for me in this spiritless machine of a city gone bad. I got through it OK, but if I'd only known. . . .

Henry Miller wrote, "The moment one gives close atten-

tion to anything, even a blade of grass, it becomes a mysterious, awesome, indescribably magnificent world in itself."

In formal monastic meals we acknowledge in chants that
food does not come to us automatically. The rice does not
grow on the end of the fork. Similarly, the buildings that sur-
round us in the city did not spring from the ground, concrete
and steel generating spontaneously out of air and desire.

Now when I go to New York or when I am on the road
teaching and find myself in a city, I am able to center myself,
aware of the complexity and wonder of my surroundings. I
was recently in the Atlanta airport, a challenge to mindfulness
if ever there was one. I have flown through Atlanta for years
and have watched that airport turn itself, with vigor, into a
mall to rival the best New Jersey has to offer. I was running
from one terminal to the next. Running, mind you, on the
moving sidewalk. I was anywhere but present. I had just left
my father's sick bed in Gainesville and was terribly worried
about him. I was on my way home where I had a dental appointment scheduled in the late afternoon. I was going to
have two (more) teeth pulled. Suffering on both ends of this
journey and I was running on a moving sidewalk. I caught
myself. I was doing what I was conditioned to do. All around
me, women and men were rushing for appointments, assigna-
tions, homecomings, and leave-takings. All of us were, in
Thich Nhat Hanh's exquisite phrase, "missing our appointments with life." I got off the sidewalk. I breathed in and
breathed out, slowly and deeply, *knowing* I was breathing in
and out. "Present moment, wonderful moment." I began to
walk slowly and mindfully through all the rushing and worry.
As artificial an environment as this was, I could see the human
effort that had gone into its construction. The girders were

created of flame, impure iron, and carbon. Real people had made them and placed them there. I could see family stories in this place of steel and fabric. Suffering went into building this place as did the joy of accomplishment. There was someone's blood in that steel.

It's difficult to walk mindfully in such an environment without feeling conspicuous and a little foolish. Sometimes it's difficult to walk mindfully in such a place without feeling a little holy. Be careful. I commend this practice to you. Thich Nhat Hanh reminds us that we don't have to be poets to see the cloud in this piece of paper. Look closely. Look for the fire. Look for the rose.

I May Not Be Much, but I'm All I Ever Think About

~~~~~~

A IS A SELFISH PROGRAM. I am in it, not for my wife or my child, but for me. I take what I need and I leave the rest. I'm here for me. This is what is true about AA.

AA is a selfless program. We are in it together. I share my experience, strength, and hope in order to help you. The newcomer is the most important person in the room. This is what is true about AA.

AA is a selfish program *and* AA is a selfless program. It is not some mixture of the two. There is nothing muddy and uncertain about it at all. AA is not a little bit of selfless and a little bit of selfish. It is, again, "perfect and complete; lacking nothing." The prayer of St. Francis says, "Make me a channel of thy peace." This great prayer then goes on to ask that the supplicant be granted the ability to *do* that which she herself most *needs*. She wishes to bring hope to despair, harmony to discord, and light to shadows. Humbly, she asks to be able to forgive rather than to be forgiven and to love rather than to be loved. She acknowledges that by dying she awakens to eternal life.

In my early days without alcohol, I was fretful about all this. "Which is it? selfishness or selflessness?" I needed certainty. I think that uncertainty and ambiguity are more threatening to me than the reality of impermanence. I'm going to die. That's certain. But in the meantime, I insist on the concrete. I didn't want mystery unless it was only something to talk about. True mystery, like true knowledge of the self, was terrifying to me. If I couldn't get the answer, I was going to fall into some endless abyss. Existential chaos loomed just ahead, beyond the crack in the sidewalk. I am more comfortable with ambiguity now. I have had a glimpse, through Zen practice, of the interpenetration of all phenomena. Hammocks swing between the stars and I am free.

As I reflect on these words, I am uncomfortably aware of my teacher, John Daido Loori, sitting on my shoulder and saying, "If you think it is one over the other, you miss it!" Then, "If you think it is both selfish and selfless, you miss it!" More forcefully, "If you think you see it, you miss it."

In my drinking and drugging days, everything that happened was about me. I felt that everyone I knew thought about me several times a day. My concerns and my needs were paramount. When I was struck with an emotion, it filled the universe and demanded attention. It would not end. There was no perspective. If sad, I would be sad forever. If happy, I was enraptured. Me, me, me, me, me was the cry.

When I first sobered up, I fantasized a life of service. I would selflessly give myself to the suffering alcoholic. Like many who have been sober for a fairly short while, I began to collect "pigeons"; newcomers, that is, whom I talked to by phone every day and helped through treacherous shoals of sobriety even more newly arrived upon than my own.

Two Addictions. Two attachments. One to selfishness. One to selflessness. In the recovered life, the two "inter-are." One of the vows of the Buddha Way is "Sentient Beings are numberless; I vow to save them." How arrogant! How inflated and impossible!

Yet this vow is the North Star by which I find my way. I never arrive at the North Star, but I move resolutely on the way. To save all sentient beings is to be saved by all sentient beings. In his penetrating book on the moral and ethical teachings of Buddhism, *The Heart of Being*, Daidoshi wrote:

> We've got a habitual way of dealing with the world, a way that is self-centered, that comes from our conditioning. This practice is an opportunity to turn it over and see it from all sides, an opportunity to take care of the things that need taking care of in a way that's not self-centered, that doesn't oppose this over that but sees the whole thing as an interacting totality that affects everything. It's only in this way that we can nourish and heal ourselves and the environment.

In serving you, I serve myself. In serving myself, I serve you. It is neither selfish nor selfless. It is a whole new way of being that doesn't need such distinctions. What is most telling to me in Daido's commentary above is the phrase ". . . and the environment." There is a totality of healing that begins as I begin to heal. As I heal, you heal. As we heal, the family heals. As the family heals, the community heals. As the community heals, the great earth is healed. As the great earth is healed, I am healed.

BREATHING ROOM

This one is suggested by Thich Nhat Hanh.

When your telephone rings, don't answer it right away. Use the ringing as a bell of mindfulness. Stay where you are and let the phone ring three times before you go to answer it. Use this time to breathe in and breathe out. Let go of any thoughts about who is calling. When you answer the phone, smile as you say hello.

I would add: Get rid of call waiting!

Keep Coming Back

~~~~~~~~~~~~~~~~~~~~~~~~~~~~~~~~~~~~~

COMPOSING PERSONAL GATHAS

SUNDAY LUNCH AT ZEN MOUNTAIN MONAS-
TERY is a special time. Following, as it does, a week of
practice and often weekend-long workshops on Zen arts
or other aspects of practice, it is a time of relaxation and cama-
raderie. The air is charged with the joy of something seen
deeply for the first time or just the relief of not having some
idiot insistently ringing a bell at 4:45 AM to get you into the
zendo on time. There is a huge feast of spaghetti with sauce,
either vegetarian or nonvegetarian.

On one such Sunday, I ate lunch with a friend who was
a resident at the monastery and a longtime member of Alcoholics Anonymous. After two heaping platefuls of the nonvegetarian pasta, salad, and two purloined chocolate cookies, I
got up to leave and said to my friend, "Keep coming back,"
an AA cliché meant to remind us never to leave AA practice.
I then looked around and said, "You don't need to keep coming back, you're already here." She laughed and said, "Oh, no.
Especially here I need to be reminded." What she meant, I
believe, is that the distractions from the present moment are

particularly strong at a place where study of the self is the overreaching commitment. It is easy in such a place to slip into resentment at "some idiot" who wakes you in the morning, or at the severity of practice. It is also a breeding place for spiritual materialism, a sense of holier than thou.

A *gatha* is a short verse, often poetic and rich with images, which can "bring us back to life," in the words of Thich Nhat Hanh. This is so very important. When we are not living in the present moment, we miss so much. When the bird calls, we miss it. When the child cries for help, we miss it. When our lover touches us, we miss it. When the gods offer gifts we fail to see them. Gathas have the power to renew our lives at every moment. These are verses of mindful living.

Here are a few gathas from the book *Gathas for Everyday Life* by the Chinese master Du Ti. The modern translation is by Thich Nhat Hanh. Although the verses are slanted toward monastic life, they carry a powerful lay message.

Waking Up

Waking up this morning, I smile.
Twenty four brand-new hours are before me.
I vow to live each moment fully
and to look at all beings
with the eyes of compassion

Turning on the Water

Water flows from high in the mountains.
Water runs deep in the Earth.
Miraculously, water comes to us,
and sustains all life.

Washing My Hands

Water flows over these hands.
May I use them skillfully
to preserve our precious planet.

Brushing My Teeth

Brushing my teeth and rinsing my mouth,
I vow to speak purely and lovingly.
When my mouth is fragrant
with right speech,
a flower blooms in the garden of my heart.

Hearing the Bell

Listen, listen
this wonderful sound
brings me back
to my true self.

Robert Aitken, Roshi, is the founder and director of the Diamond Sangha, a Zen Buddhist community in Hawaii. He is the author of several important books on practice, most notably for me *The Mind of Clover* and *Taking the Path of Zen*. In 1992 Parallax Press published his book *The Dragon Who Never Sleeps—Verses for Zen Buddhist Practice*. Go get a copy. Aitken Roshi gave us this book because, as he puts it, "monks and nuns of the T'ang period had no gathas for noticing a billboard advertising Jim Beam Kentucky Sour Mash Whiskey. As lay Western Buddhists, however, we pick our way daily through an agglomeration of compelling reminders to pamper ourselves and serve no one else." His gathas are written in the formal style of the *Hua Yen Ching* or Sk. *Avatamsaka Sutra*, the noblest of the Mahayana scriptures, which has four-line stanzas with one line always a "vow with all beings." These elegant poems are wonderful reminders of the interrelationship of all beings *right now* in the culture of noise and acquisition. Below are a few examples that speak directly to me.

When I'm moved to complain about others
I vow with all beings
to remember that karma is endless
and it's loving that leads to love.

When the children get cranky and whiny
I vow with all beings
to stop what I'm doing and cuddle
and show them I know times are tough.

When the dentist takes up his drill
I vow with all beings
to welcome the pain and discomfort
as doors to a steady mind.

In a paranoid cycle of thoughts
I vow with all beings
to enjoy a cold glass of water
and step out to look at the sky.

When I reach for the keys to my car
I vow with all beings
to consider alternate transport:
feet, or a bike, or the bus.

Watching gardeners label their plants
I vow with all beings
to practice the old horticulture
and let plants identify me.

I encourage you to write your own gatha. The form is simple enough. Line one states the situation. "Stuck in traf-

fic." "Caressing my lover." "When offering my opinions."
"When the children are fighting." "When filled with desire
for more and more things at the Mall." For our uses here, let's
make it, "When I start explaining it all." Then, if you wish to
follow the formal style you can "vow with all beings," a profound promise to acknowledge the interpenetration of all
things and the most exquisite example I know of the desire to
manifest good for all beings. Then "with humility as your
guide," you state the resolution, the simple self-deflator. It is
important here to avoid the ironic and self-damning attitude
so prevalent in Alcoholics Anonymous. This is no place to say,
for example, "I will remember it's my best thinking that got
me here." Remember that it *was* your best thinking that got
you here. There was that one moment of profound insight
that said, perhaps, "I don't have to drink" that got you here.
Another more positive statement would be "That I will notice
my feet / and let the path be the teacher."

I encourage you to find collections of these little poems
and write down and carry with you the ones that speak most
directly to you. If there is one you simply cannot tolerate,
please stick that one in your pocket and look at it often. More
important I urge you to write your own. This is the spirit of
the Tenth Step, filtered through two thousand years of wisdom and bounced off of the life we live right here, right now.
"Continued to take personal inventory and when we saw we
were off the path, promptly corrected our course."

> When I am tempted to stop my work
> I vow with all beings
> to consult with my teacher, that lazy one
> to see the value of what I do.

How to Wash Dishes

~~~~~~~~~~~~~~~~~~~~~~~~~~~~~~

W HEN I FIRST GOT SOBER, I was crazed and off center. I barely slept for the first several months and couldn't concentrate on anything. Work was impossible. I was employed as a senior editor at a large publishing company, but between anxiety, ongoing detoxification from alcohol and cocaine, and a chimerical aphasia, I was incapable of doing my job. I went to AA meeting after AA meeting, once setting an all time personal best of attending seven meetings in one day. In the first ninety days I went to over 250 meetings. I lived and breathed "recovery." There was nothing more important to me than to never feel again the way I had felt on a daily basis for the previous seven years. I had no old friends left and making new ones was difficult.

I sat in AA meetings with my mind wandering from distant past to endless future and from the moment just passed to the dreaded lonesome night just ahead. I often sat in open meetings planning my menu for that night, never hearing a word that anyone said. I cannot tell you to this day the content of the remarks of any speaker I heard during the first thirty days of my new life. I knew that I needed to find something to do to occupy my mind for at least a few minutes in the late evenings. That was the hardest time for me. I had broken up with a woman I thought I loved only six months or so before I sobered up. I was, as well, still obsessed with a

love affair gone horribly wrong during my last three months in San Francisco, before moving to New York in 1982. These failures and betrayals haunted me and they never loomed larger than when the sky began to darken and I was alone in my tiny two rooms on East Seventy-seventh Street. I felt mocked by the happy couples I saw on the street and in meetings.

Today I know that if it had not been those events, there would have been others. My psyche was torn adrift. The world was not familiar and there seemed nothing to hold on to but the rawest wounds of the recent past. I needed peace, if only for a few moments, and didn't know how to find it. I couldn't pray then because the word *God* stuck in my throat and I knew nothing useful about meditation at the time. I often went to a late meeting on Seventy-ninth street and then just wandered Manhattan for hours until I thought I was tired enough to sleep for at least a few hours.

One evening, late in November of 1984, I had finished dinner and was getting ready to wash the pans and dishes. The little sink was full of hot water and soap bubbles. The light from the window onto the air shaft was falling across the bubbles and I noticed the sheen and play of colors there. I watched for a moment or two and then set out, very consciously, to wash those dishes in a different way from that to which I was accustomed. I piled the dirty dishes, pots and silverware on the kitchen table, only a foot or so behind me. I carefully took each piece separately and washed it thoroughly, feeling the heat and the viscous quality of the water. When the water began to get cold, I would add more hot water. I don't remember exactly but I feel confident that it took at least twenty minutes to wash and dry those few dishes from my solitary meat and potatoes dinner. I knew enough to realize that what I had done was a form of meditation. I also knew that what appealed to me so was how ordinary an endeavor it was. There was no temple incense burning; I hadn't chanted over the forks or prayed over the skillet. I had simply washed my dishes. The ordinariness of it was overwhelming. I didn't need to do anything "special" to meditate. I only had to wash my dishes. From that night to this moment, the time I spend washing dishes has been my most personal time. I feel the water, the soap, and the food scraps as the gifts I know they are.

This was how I began the practice of meditation. Years later I read in Thich Nhat Hanh's book *The Miracle of Mindfulness* that novice monks in Vietnamese Zen monasteries are assigned the job of washing dishes when they first arrive. It is not so easy a job for them as it was for me, with all my hot water and Joy. They only have cold water and sand and rice husks to use for scraping the pans. How fortunate I was to have Joy.

There is some useful activity that you perform every day that can become your meditation practice or an occasion for mindfulness. Doing the laundry mindfully will get the mind clean. I once lived with someone who insisted on thoroughly cleaning her apartment every Saturday. Every Saturday. There was one particular pigeon-hole desk that I would just as soon have used for kindling. Those tiny holes! If you have some piece of furniture like that, clean it mindfully.

The important thing is to notice what you are doing. When you are cleaning your dishes, don't let anyone else into the kitchen. Particularly dismiss quickly those people who come in from distant places, perhaps the grave, to watch and comment on your dishwashing. Your lasagna pan is none of their business. When you are cleaning your dishes, you can put aside tomorrow's meeting or tonight's television program that you must watch. How important is it really? Washing your dishes can be the most important thing in your life while you are doing it. It is, in fact, the only thing in your life at that moment. The rest is your mind chattering at you. Look carefully at that teacup.

When washing your dishes, just wash your dishes. Everything else will take care of itself.

Already Broken

~~~~~~~~~~~~~~~~~~~~~~~~~~~~~~~~~~~~~~

GOD IN THE WOUNDS

To set up what you like against what you dislike—
this is the disease of the mind.

—SENG-T'SAN

I N   H I S   C H A L L E N G I N G   A N D   L U C I D   B O O K   *Thoughts Without A Thinker,* Mark Epstein tells a story about an encounter with the meditation master Achaan Chaa at his monastery in Thailand. He recounts that on his first morning there, after a round of walking the countryside with the resident monks, carrying begging bowls and creating a titillation among the children, these strange Western monks tagging along with their Thai brethren, they had breakfast and then were given an audience with the teacher. As Epstein tells it, they sat for some time, wanting to ask just the right question of this acute and patient master. Finally they asked, "What are you really talking about? What do you mean by 'eradicating craving'?" Picking up a glass of water, he answered, "You see this goblet. To me it is already broken. I enjoy it; I drink out of it. It holds my water admirably, sometimes even reflecting the sun in beautiful patterns. If I should tap it, it has a lovely ring to it. But when I put this glass on a shelf and the wind knocks it over or my elbow brushes it off the table and it falls to the ground and shatters, I say, 'Of course.' But when I understand that this glass is already broken, every moment with it is precious."

Mark Epstein is a fortunate man to have sat with such a teacher, and his book reflects his own learning, wisdom, and compassion. When I read, or heard, the words "already broken," I felt rather than merely knew this great teaching. Epstein writes about the already broken *self*, "this self that you take to be so real." Certainly that is the case, but what speaks to me more deeply here is the understanding of impermanence and the sweet, dear, and fragile nature of every relationship. It is my opinion of my relationships that causes all the trouble. This should be like that or that should be like this. By relationship, of course, I mean my wife, children, friends, co-workers; but I mean as well this computer and that pin oak out there that has just dropped a massive dead limb across the road.

It is also only in relationship that we are healed and that we have our awakening. There is nothing other than relationship. What can you show me that is not relationship? From the *Tao-te Ching*, here is Lao Tse on the reality of compassion (with emphasis added):

Simple in actions and in thoughts,
you return to the source of being.
Patient with both friends and enemies,

you accord with the way things are.
Compassionate toward yourself,
you reconcile all beings in the world.

I want to relate a story of a reconciliation that had its beginning on a black cushion in a dark meditation hall. I needed to look at something that I would not look at until the pain of not looking was so great that I couldn't look away. My experience over many years of freedom from chemicals has shown me that I am not alone. Many of us are plagued by at least one relationship that we can't set straight. This is gravely dangerous business. If we can't get that one straight, the rest of them suffer.

"Resentment is the number one offender," according to Bill Wilson. Self-activated hatred is not an unusual experience for many addicts and alcoholics. Resentment becomes a way of being. Without it, we are left with no one to blame. At another level, without resentment our monkey minds do not have anything to do. There is yet another empty place, another "god-shaped hole" that needs to be filled. It is habit of mind to fill it with judgment, criticism, aversion, or resentment. This is a grave situation. For those of us with alcoholism, it can lead back to the bar. Resentment leads to one of the most twisted and damning of all alcoholic ploys: "I'll show you, I'll hurt me." Forgiveness is the way out, but it is my experience that the only true forgiveness, finally, is that which is preceded by insight and fueled by compassion.

The story I want to tell concerns a young man in my life who is very troubling. Not troubled, troubl*ing*. His daimon is a demanding one who has yet to show its hand. Several therapists have had a go at this young man over the short course of his life thus far. The daimon is obdurate and no "cure" has been forthcoming. He is bright, clever, and able to show a penetrating understanding of the way people work. It is an understanding I can appreciate. In me, it nearly progressed to paranoia during my days of addiction and often showed up as a deep unwillingness to trust others. I thought I could see through to motivations, in truth, and became overly afraid. This is not yet true of this lad, although he is shy for other reasons. He has no friends as you and I understand friendship. He isolates. He speaks his truth inappropriately without understanding the consequences, occasionally with hilarious results. In his presence, the emperor is clearly buck naked. A brief example: He was once at a family party and the wealthy patriarch of one clan represented there was dominating the conversation with ruminations on his theatrically perceived but hardly imminent death. He asked with great drama what he should be doing to prepare for this great event. There was a silence born, I suspect, of embarrassment and the deep desire not to offend. My little friend spoke clearly into this silence and suggested, guilelessly, that this old gentleman should probably get to writing his will. Quickly.

I am writing a charming portrait of this young man, partly born of my reluctance to admit to how very difficult it was for me to live with him. He is charming but he touched off in me incredible anger and resentment. I owe it to him not to give details here. Two of the gifts of the substance-free life are loyalty and prudence. His troubles are his own. It is my trouble that I am telling you about. It was simple. There were times when I couldn't be around him. There were times when I looked for someone to blame for the despair I alone seemed to feel. Never had anyone affected me this way and that stew of emotions was further poisoned by the shame I felt about them. I tried everything I knew to get help. Nothing worked and the dilemma deepened. I was no longer just occasionally angry as when he kept everyone waiting or acted inappropriately, with that same lack of guile that was so refreshing in other situations. I was always angry and resentful and I saw no way out. The only way left then, was IN.

Step Ten of the program of Alcoholics Anonymous suggests that anger is an "occasional luxury of more balanced people" and should be left to those more capable of handling it. That is not my experience at all. In this world where simple manners and civility can be expressed only with the oily patina of post-modern irony, I fail to see many folks who are more balanced than those who have taken a close look at their addictions and made the inspiring effort to overcome them. Anger, noticed and acknowledged but not expressed, is no luxury. It is human. The danger is when anger is held, nurtured, and slips ever so subtly, into hate. The second of the Three Poisons is called in some translations "anger," in others "aversion." My preference is to call it "hatred." Greed, hatred, and delusion drive us all when the spiritual life is left unattended. And I was joining in the march as I began to hate this innocent person. I had to abandon every idea I had about how to get out of this mess. In AA we hear that we should "turn it over," that is, let God handle it. I'm not so good at that but I have a well-developed knack for "dropping it." The result is the same. I gave up. I knew that there had to be a solution and I realized I didn't know what it could possibly be.

Shortly thereafter I was listening to a tape of Thich Nhat Hanh in a lecture on love and compassion. At one point, he said words to this effect: If you are having trouble with your spouse, then it doesn't matter why Bodhidharma came to the East. The reference is to one of many koans, which are impenetrable riddles that cannot be answered with reason or logic and that are used in Zen training to develop insight and awakening. The koan in this case is "Why did Bodhidharma come to the East?" Thich Nhat Hanh's point is that Zen practice is about the real stuff of our lives and when we are in turmoil we can use practice, here seated meditation, as a way to clarity.

At the time of my personal turmoil around this young man, I had been a Zen student and practitioner for several years and had begun formal koan study with my teacher John Daido Loori and, subsequently, with Bonnie Myotai Treace at the Fire Lotus Zendo in New York City. I knew just enough to see that Thây had offered the solution. Sit with this problem. Stop thinking about it and just sit. As I write those words I hear the voice of Daido in the still meditation hall. At full volume with just a hint of baritone tremolo, each vowel elongated, each consonant rasped, I hear JUST SIT!

In the spirit of the Eleventh Step, I "sought through prayer and meditation to improve my conscious contact with God." That is, I sought to look more deeply at this problem without over-rationalizing it, without discursive, linear thought. So, the next morning as I sat zazen I simply said to myself, "What About It?", meaning my relationship with this lad (prayer?). As in koan work, I had swallowed the question to let my deeper consciousness (God?) work on it. The question continued to torment me, but my relationship to it had changed. Frustration had been replaced by faith. "What About It?" "What About It?"

Weeks later I headed off to Zen Mountain Monastery in Mt. Tremper, New York, the home of the Mountain and Rivers Order, for a week-long *sesshin*—literally, "gathering the heartmind"—which is a period of intensive meditation practice with up to six hours of seated meditation a day, interspersed with work periods, formal meals, and dharma talks (lectures) by the teacher. The days are long and the work is hard. In my experience the rewards are great and always unpredictable. For example, on an earlier occasion I was driving back to New Jersey from one such retreat, legs and hands still cramped from the long sitting, listening to an Elvis Presley CD from the complete '50s masters collection. The song "I Was the One" came on and I lost it. I began crying, spontaneously and without warning, and had to pull off the freeway to just let it rip. To this day I have no idea where that came from, although a little voice keeps whispering, "It's about Sara Sue Phelps," my girlfriend at the time of Elvis's early ascendancy.

The monastery is 120 miles from my home. On this occasion, as I drove up for the sesshin, you could have measured the trip another way by saying it took one gas stop, four dunkin' donuts (two maple, two chocolate), a slice of plain pizza, and a large coffee with milk and sugar. By the time I hit my cushion in the zendo that night I was in a carbohydrate stupor. The monastery is a forbidding place in the best of circumstances. One friend refers to it as the Dark Tower. It smells of incense and sautéed onions, with an overlay of woodsmoke year round. Not a good place to be riding a sugar crash. In addition to this metabolic disaster, I had a terrible cough, irritated by the incense smoke and the cold. During one break from sitting for *kinhin*, which is rapid walking meditation, a senior monastic pulled me aside and told me there was a stash of cough drops in a desk downstairs. So it was that bad, was it? Other people are coughing, why single me out?

The day ended, my metabolism was wrecked, sleep was difficult and waking in the morning even harder. I once heard the writer and Zen practitioner Jan Wilhelm van de Wetering describe the start of the monastic day as, "Some idiot comes knocking on your door at three in the morning." True. You bolt out of bed and must be seated in the zendo twenty minutes later. I did and was. I also knew that there was still some time left before formal sitting began. What I did not remember (don't forget the donuts) was that formal sitting was preceded by a walk through by the Abbot at which time everyone is expected to be seated. My coughing was terrible so I got up, bowed to my cushion, walked rapidly out of the zendo, turning at the door to bow once more, and scurried downstairs to cop some cough drops. I took one and stuffed several more into the capacious sleeves of my robe. I ran back up the stairs and was about to bow to reenter the zendo when Ryushin, the monitor and a senior monastic and, I thought, my friend, bellowed out "Too late!" Surely he misunderstood. He must have seen me on my cushion before. I started to enter once more. "Too Late!" Ryushin came to me and motioned that I should sit in the corridor separated from the Zendo by a low wall. Forty other students were seated properly, in four long rows, two facing two, and I alone had been sent to the back of the class!

The Abbot entered and the first thing he saw was me. He made his rounds, passing all the students, who bowed; I am certain he passed my so very empty cushion with contempt and disdain. Leaving the zendo he passed directly to my right. I bowed but could not see if he even returned it.

The thirty-five-minute period passed slowly. I was mortified. I was coughing, although much less, and had a sugar hangover. I tried to "be" the mortification. To "be" the cough and the hangover. I sat with it. When the period ended I could get back to my cushion to begin another.

As I bowed to the cushion and began to fold myself into zazen posture, I vowed to myself to use this one period completely. To use it and to be used up totally by it. Mortification had turned to anger to ferocious resolve. I would, by all the buddhas and boddhisattvas, sit like no one had ever sat before. I remember nothing about that period to this day. Suddenly, the bell rang to signal kinhin. We walked for a few minutes and then sat once more, the final period before formal breakfast, also taken in the zendo. As I sat, I made the same vow I had made in the previous period. This time it did not work. As is often the case, each period of sitting can be different. This time my monkey mind would not leave me alone. "I coughed and pissed everyone off," I thought. "I stumbled leaving the zendo. I got sent to the back of the class . . . and everyone knows it. I'm the goat. I guess there has to be one in every group."

Chatter, chatter, chatter—and every attempt to stop it failed. All the while, lurking in the background, there was "What about it? What about it?" Prayer and meditation.

All at once I became that terrible koan. For a moment I disappeared and in my place, in that cold zendo, in the light of candles before dawn, with incense and onions, I became the small boy who had become the young man who bedeviled me so. As I sat there, I knew his suffering. The best I could do then is the best I can do now to articulate that transcendent realization: "This is the way he feels all the time." My feeling of being not enough, incompetent, the goat, was transitory, but I understood that he felt that way daily. He did not fit in and he was not understood. He was lonely and apart. Bill Wilson speaks of the condition of "anxious apartness." That was it. Sitting on that cushion I vowed not to be the cause of those feelings in that young man ever again. I have not been perfect but I cannot forget that sense of deep empathy that was, for me, the only way out of hatred.

Dunkin' donuts and coffee is not the way to enlightenment. It is not necessary to become a Buddhist or to subject yourself to the sweet rigors of sesshin to empathize with the suffering of another.

Take a deep look at what is bedeviling you. The Three Poisons help to categorize the devils. Is it a problem of greed? Of hatred? Of delusion? Are you not getting what you think you should have? Is there someone or some number or class of people that is keeping you from getting what you think you should have? In my case, I thought (delusion) that I should have serenity when what I had was chaos (greed) and for this I blamed my young friend. It's easy to see how these three interpenetrate. Not one of them can stand totally alone. I Hate because I Think I should Have. For the purpose of this ongoing practice of prayer and meditation, it is useful to name one of the poisons. I hated that person. Name the problem. Take some time to become mindful. Breathing in, I know I am breathing in. Breathing out, I know I am breathing out. Present moment, only moment. Sit quietly by your altar and breathe gently. When you are calm, when monkeymind has shut up, it is time to pose the question. You will know what the specific questions are but it is most useful to let them go and just ask, "What about it?" Sit quietly for a while longer and enjoy your breathing. Finally go about your day and the days to come. The question is being worked on by your higher power. The fire of attention is focused. When you are worried and upset about your situation, breathe in and out and ask, "What about it?"

This process takes some time. I have never spontaneously gotten rid of any of the barriers between myself and others. But I have worn them down. I have come to understand the beautiful truth of "already broken." I also demand of myself that I expand my limits and celebrate the lives of people like my little friend, who is so much like me in our mutual brokenness, who point the way toward the deeper and richer self.

Lenny and the Three Stooges

~~~~~~~~~~~~~~~~~~~~~~~~~~~

FROM ANESTHESIA TO CLARITY

*The nonalcoholic world has many lessons which it might learn . . .
from the ways of AA. If we continue to operate in terms of a
Cartesian dualism of mind versus matter, we shall probably also
continue to see the world in terms of God versus man; elite versus
people; chosen race versus others; nation versus nation; and man
versus environment. It is doubtful whether a species having both an
advanced technology and this strange way of looking at its world
can endure.*

—GREGORY BATESON

M Y FRIEND LENNY TOOK his children to see what
was at the time a hit movie, ostensibly for "children of any age." Before it was halfway through,
Lenny found himself wrapped in despair. When he called and
we talked about it, he said that he was taken apart by the
realization that this piece of "entertainment," loaded with ma-
licious humor and sadistic violence, perpetrated by one child

on two adults, was seen as acceptable fare. I had taken my three oldest kids to see it just a few days before. Lizzie, then nine, had spent most of the movie holding on to my arm and looking away from the mayhem. John and Ed were sitting with friends and laughing shrilly at each instance of pain and assault. Their laughter reminded me of my own at their age, when I would sit with friends and watch the Three Stooges. I did not like what I saw. I felt, inarticulately, that this was the behavior of pitiless fools, vulgar and common. I laughed nonetheless, feeling that I had to fit in, that I was somehow in the wrong for not appreciating this witless humor. I had heard the same hollow laughter from my boys at that movie and told Lenny so, describing my juvenile response to Curly, Larry, and Moe. I threw in a reference to Jerry Lewis as well, whom I never understood and whose movies made me deeply uncomfortable as a child, as I'm sure they still would today.

Lenny was quiet for a moment and then told me that he, too, had felt uncomfortable watching the Stooges and Jerry Lewis and that, like me, he had laughed anyway, never certain whether he was missing something that others saw or understanding something that others failed to see. We continued to talk about feelings we had both had when we were younger that what was popular often seemed horrid to us and how, when alone, we would eagerly turn away from such torpid meanness.

After our conversation, I was left feeling that at least I wasn't alone in my feelings about gross and painful physical comedy. That was reward enough at the time, but the conversation wouldn't leave me. It continued to lurk, popping up from time to time and demanding greater attention than it would seem to warrant. What was it about my sorrow and

Lenny's, in response to a foolish movie seen with our children, that had such a hold on me? I couldn't dismiss it.

My understanding now is that this deep feeling was the awakening of despair. Despair, like grief, sorrow, and anger, is not an acceptable attitude in this culture. But Lenny and I were in despair. In the presence of our children we had been exposed to meanness and brutality wrapped up in pretty tinsel and passed off as holiday entertainment. This sort of artless exploitation always surrounds us, but this particular movie was the one that opened up the despair box for us both. The movie was a gift, finally. Lenny and I were left with sadness and healing.

I know that this feeling is familiar to you. Think of the times when you have wanted to shout "Stop it!" at a movie screen or the TV set. No one among us is a stranger to the dullness that overcomes the mind and spirit before the persistent violence of our culture. We don't know what to do. Some might ask why we should holler at exploitative entertainment when real children are being used as sex slaves in our cities and towns. The answer is that both of those things cause suffering. It's a matter of degree. The lesser suffering does not ennoble the greater; the greater does not excuse the lesser. *Life suffers* is the first of the Buddha's Four Noble Truths. When I make my daily vow to save all sentient beings, I do not follow this with a list of those more or less worthy of relief. I save all sentient beings by saving myself. When I say I wish to relieve suffering, I am saying that I am open to having my suffering relieved. This is not a selfish vow. At bottom, I am saying that I see no distinction between self and other. As you read this, I care for you out of care for myself and with the understanding that you and I *inter-are*. Your suffering is mine. My suffering is yours.

In the world of exploitation, I do not feel your suffering. In that dark world, grief and pain are outside of my little, illusory self. The dark twin in his deep addiction is *unfeeling*.

Alcohol is an *anesthetic*. It kills feeling. The first casualty of active addiction is not, as is often claimed, the spirit. The first casualty of ongoing addiction to *anything*, including recovery, is the imagination. The dark twin grips the mind and every creative act is squeezed through the grip of the addiction and informed by it. The thirst finds its way into every act. I have heard many alcoholics say, "I have a disease that keeps telling me I don't have a disease." Addiction clouds the imagination's looking glass and, unfeeling ourselves, we see the hangman's smile but never feel the rope. Snuff films excite. The evening news is entertainment—a savage pastiche that rings in hollow ears and, if it serves any purpose at all, only makes us feel, curiously, alive.

How do we come to? Fresh mind, by which I mean a mind that is spontaneously "honest, open, and willing." It is the unencumbered mind, free of opinion, unconditioned. When you are operating from fresh mind you go to the movie theater with no expectations *even if* you saw the movie the day before. I know that when I go into dokusan, or face-to-face teaching, with Daidoshi, he sees me with fresh mind. I may have just been in that room the day before and failed miserably in my attempt to show him "mu," but if I blunder in this new attempt, he looks at me without reference to yesterday's failure or success. "What is it" doesn't mean "What was it." "What about it" does not mean "What is the thought you had while eating your donuts yesterday"; it just means "What about it."

I have a writing desk that sits in a window in my office. It is close to the floor and the top is angled to hold a writing pad just so. In front of this desk is a *seiza* bench, usually used for meditation practice. When my mind has gone to sleep, I sit at that desk to do my work. It is a sensual and centering exercise. I smell the pencils and hear the scratch they make against the rough yellow paper. When writing at the computer, it is entirely reasonable to expect to find me listening to music, often the likes of Jimi Hendrix or Johnny Cash. But at this writing desk, I do not play music. I listen to my mind move in order to refresh it.

Please find a place to go to refresh your mind and then carry that place and that mind into your day.

Throughout this book there have been little suggestions for that refreshment. Here is one more. Right now, take a moment to breathe in and breathe out. Breathing in, I know I am honest, open, and willing; breathing out, I am awake. Breathing in, breathing out. Breathing in, I see myself as a flower; breathing out, I feel fresh.

Today is full of infinite possibilities to refresh your mind. Whenever you find yourself falling asleep or drifting into the misery of forgetfulness, awaken to one of them. The rapture is deadly. The anesthetized life is lethal. As people who have lived in anesthesia, we now embrace feeling with body, mind, and spirit. "Drunken dumbshow" is not for us.

Lenny and I sat through that witless movie and knew something was wrong. I'm pretty sure our kids did too. Conditioned mind said something different to each of us and, to each of us, it spoke through the conditioning and the rapture

of forgetfulness. For each of us as well, fresh mind was pushing through. It was fresh mind that was telling us the emperor has no clothes. Our discomfort was born of the persistence of fresh mind as it tried to overwhelm the anesthetized mind. A Zen master said that "if a man lives in forgetfulness, he dies in a dream." Fresh mind is the way to wake up. As we develop that mind, we begin to remember what we saw so clearly as children. Please enjoy your fresh mind.

Watch out for the popcorn!

BREATHING ROOM

"Mindfulness is the energy that sheds light on all things and all activities, producing the power of concentration, bringing forth deep insight and awakening."—Thich Nhat Hanh

In a moment, please put the book aside and look slowly around you. Offer blessings to everything you see. Now.

Get (It) Together

~~~~~~

P RACTICING BUDDHISTS "take refuge" daily in
what are known as the Three Jewels. I understand this
as a way of expressing humility and of acknowledging
a connection to powers "greater than myself" or to the power
of things as they are. This is not a metaphor. It is an expression of the truth.

In some traditions this connection is expressed by three
bows, often repeated many times. In others, there is a combination of bows and chanting. In the Order of Interbeing, the
connection is expressed through a chant that is part of daily
liturgical practice, either at home or in a group. Here is that
chant.

> I take refuge in the Buddha, the one who shows me the way
> in this life. Namo Buddhaya.
> I take refuge in the Dharma, the way of understanding and
> love. Namo Dharmaya.
> I take refuge in the Sangha, the community that lives in
> harmony and awareness. Namo Sanghaya.

I consider the Buddha here to be that greater self that I
am an expression of when I am living fully in the moment
and in consonance with the Twelve Steps and my Buddhist
vows. It is the Twelve Steps and the vows that, in this context,
are the dharma, while the sangha is my own chosen community.

The sangha is the focus here. No one who has turned his back on addiction has lasted long without "community," some very real "sangha that lives in harmony and awareness". In Twelve Step groups, the harmony comes from awareness and awareness comes from harmony. They co-exist and co-depend. That is, we enter the rooms in a shared awareness of "our common purpose" and that common purpose in itself *is* harmony.

This is not to say that all AA meetings, for example, are lessons in harmony. Hardly. I once personally hauled someone out of a meeting and with the help of two friends took that person to Bellevue. On many occasions I have had to sit on my hands and count to ten many times over in order not to let the group know how "wrong" they were. The "tradition lawyers" don't want anything but booze discussed, while some of us think that talking about alcohol is as clear an example of "Been there, done that, got the T-shirt" as we'll ever need. We want to talk about our lives after booze. There are dead words and live words in AA meetings as anywhere else. If you come to me with troubles and I give you advice or spout dogma, those are dead words. When I tell you what I felt and did in a similar situation, right from my heart/mind— Live!

I once got a phone message from a friend who was away from New York and had gone to a meeting, in a state that begins and ends with a vowel, where he was directly told that he had to "get God or get out." My friend was only a few months' sober and this silliness scared him—a fear that found expression in vitriol. He used up my entire message tape, fifteen minutes worth, and didn't even leave a number where I could call him back. He didn't need to. He's still sober twelve years later, vitriol or no, God or no. Sure, it gets nasty and silly in the rooms, but the underlying common purpose, "to stay sober and to help other alcoholics to achieve sobriety," is a bedrock of harmony. This is a sangha that works.

At the end of the WinterHeart Retreat at the Hazelden Renewal center in February of 1997, the first Ordinary Recovery retreat held at such a place, a spontaneous ceremony occurred to surprise and delight us all. I had a small bell that I had used in every retreat up to that time and that, through subterfuge, I had gotten everyone who had attended those retreats to hold at one time or another. On this day I gave it up, saying only that there was a time to let go, lighten up, and move on with everything we do. I then touched the bell, with its little cushion and "inviter" to my forehead, and gave it to Patrick S. from Madison, Wisconsin. Pat was there with five friends who were attending a retreat for the first time; it was his second. No words were said as I passed it on to him, but after I had sat back down and collected myself, I told him to use it well.

Pat and I talked afterward. I told him that I had envisioned him starting an AA meeting based on the model we had created that week in Minnesota. He said, "We're way ahead of you. We had already planned it and I was thinking this morning that we needed a bell." They have it and I am certain that the meeting is going strong today. On behalf of Pat's group in Wisconsin and of Plum Village, where it had its genesis, I want to offer you that new meeting format. It is a combination of practices that were originally developed for community meetings and in tea ceremonies in the Order of Interbeing. Although I put it together for Twelve Step meetings, it will work equally well for family get togethers or dedicated group meetings. Try it for business meetings and strategy sessions. Use it when you're talking about report cards or planning vacations. The format here will conform to the needs of Twelve Step meetings, as that is the focus of the book. Don't be put off.

The room for such a meeting should be a simple one, if possible, with chairs and cushions arranged in a circle. There is nothing inherently spiritual about sitting on the floor, and sometimes just doing so can create an unfortunate veneer of "holiness" that detracts from the connectedness and simplicity so necessary in these meetings. Chairs are fine. On the other hand, if you can provide cushions for everyone and they are used humbly, there is a sense of "getting down to business." If there are children in your group, then sitting on the floor helps put everyone on the same level. There should be a low table or a small rug in the middle of the room to hold a bell and any other objects that you find useful. A vase of fresh flowers or other reminders of the present moment can go there. One person should be designated ahead of time as the bell master. That person's only job is to signal the beginning and end of the meeting by inviting another bell than the one on the table or rug to sound. He should invite the bell to ring three times to begin the meeting and twice to end it.

Before the meeting begins, everyone sits in silence. This is the time to get centered. Leave the office. Put aside the worries that lurk just outside the room. As in a "breathing room," this is a holy place, made holy entirely by the activities of the people who are in it. The sacredness here is not imposed; it grows. When the bell master begins the meeting, everyone continues to sit in silence. If the format or focus of the meeting needs to be explained, the bell master does so now. If the entire meeting goes ahead without one word being spoken for the duration, then let it do just that. There needs to be agreement on this point. If there is nothing to say, then say it.

It is pretty unlikely, however, that no one will have anything to say. When someone wants to speak, they do a seated bow, which is returned by everyone in the room. They then go pick up the bell. Returning to their seat, they continue to hold the bell while they share their concern. The bell is never rung. It is important that no one else speak. Everyone must listen carefully, with an open mind. When the person is finished, they return the bell to the table, go back to their seat, and do another seated bow. This is, again, answered by everyone. The group sits in silence until another person wishes to speak. This continues for the agreed-upon time. When the bell master ends the meeting, the meeting is over.

One variant on this format can be to have something to eat and drink during the meeting. Drinks and food are passed from a server to each person who wishes something. The teacup, for example, is passed along by every person between the server and the one being served. This is done in silence until everyone is served.

This type of meeting brings silence and respect to what can otherwise be a noisy and disjointed situation. It is my experience from participating in such meetings that the quiet and mutual caring deepens the long-term effect.

If you start a meeting like this, for any purpose, please let me know about it by writing me in care of my publisher.

BREATHING ROOM

If you bring forth what is within you, what you bring forth
will save you. If you do not bring forth what is within you,
what you do not bring forth will destroy you.—*Jesus*

To study the Buddha way is to study the self. To study
the self is to forget the self. To forget the self is to be enlightened by the 10,000 things.—*Zen master Dogen*

Having had a spiritual awakening as the result of these
steps, we tried to carry this message to alcoholics and practice
these principles in all our affairs.—*Step Twelve of Alcoholics
Anonymous*

The Healing Buddha

~~~~~~~~~~~~~~~~

INTIMACY AND THE
COMMUNITY OF STORIES

D
URING THE WINTER OF 1987, I was sober and
in trouble with my alcoholism. I had been sober for
three years at the time and my life had improved in
ways that I could never have imagined. I was free of the desire
to drink and felt that I was seeing the reality of what many
members of AA call "the promises." The "Big Book" of Alcoholics Anonymous says—promises—that there will come a
time when:

> We are going to know a new freedom and a new happi-
> ness. We will not regret the past nor wish to shut the
> door on it. We will comprehend the word serenity and
> we will know peace. No matter how far down the scale
> we have gone, we will see how our experience can bene-
> fit others. That feeling of uselessness and self-pity will
> disappear. We will lose interest in selfish things and gain
> interest in our fellows. Self-seeking will slip away. Our
> whole attitude and outlook upon life will change. Fear
> of people and of economic insecurity will leave us. We
> will intuitively know how to handle situations which

used to baffle us. We will suddenly realize that God is doing for us what we could not do for ourselves.

My understanding was clouded by my desire. I was too good, too enraptured, too proud. This was the legendary "pink cloud" that is the lair of both the gods and the devils, a treacherous place. I had thought my way there and my arrival was premature. The Zen master says that when you arrive at the top of the hundred-foot pole, you step off. I was clinging to the rapture and swaying in the wind of my own pride and self-involvement.

I stunk of recovery.

I knew something was wrong. I was tired of listening to myself at AA meetings and was becoming increasingly irritated with people who felt differently than I did about, for just one example, God. The fulcrum tipped when I was at a morning meeting and listened, seething, to a young woman talk about how God was directing her life. Part of that direction was that she ignore some serious legal problems and quit her job. These were ways far too mysterious for me to comprehend. It was not what she said that mattered, however, it was how I reacted to what she said. I left that meeting feeling empty. There was a hole in me that nothing could fill. I hated this God and all his works. And for the first and I hope the last time since June 23, 1984, I wanted to drink. Alcoholism and the cure for alcoholism had moved outside of myself. I saw a battle with the bottle and was locked in a deeper battle with some alien self. I had disengaged from my alcoholism, using this random incident as the lever. That is what I know now. What I knew then was that I was in trouble. Buddhist practice was just ahead of me, but I couldn't see it yet.

I stayed in this awful state for several weeks. One morning I was walking home after a meeting with a friend who had been sober for about ten years. He lived in Queens but came to Manhattan early every day to work in his own window-washing business. His name was Joe. I haven't seen him for years now, but I'm pretty sure he's still doing well. I was telling him how I felt—that I was sick of AA but afraid of drinking, that all the stuff I was hearing about God made me feel like an outsider and yet that without converting to this fundamentalist view I was doomed. Joe listened as we walked down Lexington from Eighty-sixth Street to Sixty-seventh. I ranted. He listened. Finally he said, "I don't know what you can do about all that. I don't believe in God either, but I do know I'm an alcoholic. Don't forget that." We said good-bye at the corner of Sixty-seventh and Lex. I went on to my apartment. The dam had broken and the fear and despair of the previous few weeks was gone. His *turning phrase*, "Don't forget that," had done it for me. I embraced my alcoholism. In Zen parlance, I had *become* my alcoholism once more. There was no separation. I was intimate with alcoholism.

Joe had given me the gift of listening. The Boddhisattva Avalokiteshvara is known as the Bodhisattva of Compassion and her name is evoked in Vietnamese Zen ceremonies in order that we may "learn your way of listening in order to help relieve the suffering in the world." Joe gave me the gift of listening and over the years I have learned that listening is the energy that drives community, story, and healing. The reality of the sober life is the ability to listen deeply, without fear or judgment. The listener cooperates with the one being listened to. They are totally co-dependent. Like illness and medicine, they heal each other.

Throughout this book, I have allowed occasional

glimpses of my greatest regret. Here it is, straight out. I was separated from my daughter for sixteen years. I didn't know where she was and I was afraid to try to find her. The few times I did, I backed off when a meeting seemed imminent. There was a hole in my heart that was just her size.

Each of us has that one hole that seems unfillable. The wound is where God enters, according to Marion Woodman. Look closely at your wound. It has already hurt you. Now it can heal you if you will let it. If you let it, the healing will heal unknown others.

My father was a good and gentle man, but he had demons about him much of his life. I loved him deeply. He saw his faults in me and I think that hurt him. We were estranged by our suffering and shame for many years. I collapsed while Dad was still standing. Dad put that awful pain away somewhere and shared his experience and hope with me when I needed it most. I called him when I first quit drinking. During our long talk he told me that the only regret that he ever had about his father was that they could never talk about their shared problem with alcohol and that he did not want me to have that regret after he died.

For the next few years, I would call Dad and often begin the conversation by saying "I need to talk about alcohol." Even over the long-distance wires I could hear him shift his attention fully to me. I would talk about the most inane unsettling things and Dad would just listen. He didn't give me advice, he didn't judge. He just listened with all his heart/mind and I began to heal. So did he, I believe, so intense was our bond.

During that time I got a letter from my daughter. This was only the second one. Sixteen years preceded the first and that one had arrived three months after I had found her address and written her. In this second remarkable letter, she asked me if I had a problem with alcohol, because she thought she did, and if I did would I be willing to help her? I wrote her a long letter in which I told her the story of my addiction and recovery. (I was about two years sober at the time.) I ended by telling her what my father had said about his father. I told her that, like my Dad, I never wanted her to regret not being able to talk to me.

We still talk. My daughter has been sober for ten years at this writing. In her early years, she called me a lot. Her trust inspired me to keep my mouth shut. Her insistence taught me not to give advice. We teach each other in our listening.

Such stories as this have ripples. Healing reaches to places we can't see until someone shines the light on them.

In the spring of 1996, I participated in several sesshins at Zen Mountain Monastery. I was preparing to do *jukai*, the formal ceremony of becoming a Buddhist, and wanted to be sure I was doing the right thing and that I was grounded in my practice. At the end of one of these sesshins I felt particularly enriched by the experience. Doors had opened where previously I had seen only blank walls. The rapture of the hungry ghost and the years of anesthesia had worn down, diminished to a point I had not known before. I ate lunch outside, at a picnic table in the warming sun. I had chosen to sit with my friend Fusho, a monastic at Zen Mountain Monastery, with whom I had always felt a particular closeness. We had never talked that much and when we did it was usually either wondrously funny banter or Zen gossip. The connection was there, nonetheless, and we both felt it. We sat in the quiet of the surrounding mountains and talked the talk of getting to know one another. I asked where she was from and when she named a town in Tennessee just a few miles from Medon, I thought I had found the reason for our empathy.

I asked how she happened to be from there. Why had her family chosen such a place and how had she come such a long way since? Fusho is a pediatric surgeon and medical ethicist, and I had a foolish idea that no kid from a small town in Tennessee could come such a long distance. Fusho sat with my barrage of questions for a few minutes and then began telling me a story. I have her permission to tell it to you.

It is a story of a little girl whose father was an abusive drunk. She spoke of her sadness, the universal sadness of the unfathered child. She told me that her father left when she was four and she didn't know where he was for sixteen years. Their reconciliation was troubled, but she knew she loved him. She had felt abandoned and, worse, that she had deserved to be abandoned. She spoke quietly but with great power. I sat in silence. We were sitting next to each other, facing the looming back of the monastery a hundred yards away.

The afternoon slipped by as she told me the details of her story. My daughter's story. My story. When she finished I told her the story of another drunken father, one who left his daughter for sixteen years. Many of the details were the same. Neither story is finished.

When I finished, Fusho said that all she had ever wanted her father to say was that when he was young he had done some terrible things and that he was sorry. I looked at her for the first time then. There were tears on her face and her cheeks were bright red. I will always have such gratitude for her courage and trust.

I told her the end of the story of me and my daughter. I talked about the tentative reconciliation and all the attempts to rationalize and blame that I went through. Then I said that a day came when I told my daughter that I had done some terrible things when I was young and that I was sorry.

Fusho and I sat for a while longer. I think we talked a bit more, but I don't remember what we talked about. I went into the kitchen to get some more spaghetti and when I got back to the picnic table, we just sat in silence for a while. There was quite a crowd at that little table. She finally had to go and when we stood and hugged, it was a crowded hug.

My father died just a few months later, on August 27, 1996, at 11:20 at night. He would not close his eyes even as the tears came. He smiled gently just before his breath ended. He was eighty-four years old. He left an unfinished story that will continue to grow endlessly, never becoming mere history if I can help it. Dad's death has added to my life. Now that he is gone, nothing of him is missing.

I went to see Dad two days after his death. He was to be cremated, so his body was untouched by makeup or any grotesquerie meant to suggest life. He was so white, his long white hair hanging loose over the pillow. His face was unlined, his left eye not completely closed, caught in mid-wink. He was on a gurney, covered by a light blanket, wheeled into a big brown room. He dominated the room in his profound immobility. I knelt by the gurney first, rested my hands on it and looked at him. He seemed to be sweating, intense in the effort of the in-between, but it was only condensation in this warm room after the cold of the freezer. After a few minutes, I sat back into zazen, Zen seated meditation, half closed my eyes and quietly breathed "mu," the Japanese syllable meaning, literally, "nothing, not, nothingness, un-, is not, has not" but holding deeper meaning for me and many Zen practitioners. It was important to me, at a level not then understood and only glimpsed now, to be with my father in his death. I sat for some time, then stood and went close to him. I brushed his hair back, half expecting him to wince from the sudden contact with this world he had left. I held my hand against his forehead for a moment, then kissed my forefinger and held it to his lips.

I did three full bows, forehead to floor, hands raised palms up above the head, followed by one half bow, said "thank you," turned my back and walked away. I didn't mean to look back, but I did, just at the door. From that angle, his head and profile dominated my view. He hadn't moved. A sob extinguished a bellow at the back of my throat. I left in silence, bleary-eyed and sad. My daughter called that afternoon and comforted me.

The next day, Dad was to be cremated. I pressured the director of the funeral home until she finally agreed, reluctantly and apologetically, to let me see Dad in the furnace. The furnace, properly a "retort," was a Crawford C-1000, which burns for six hours at temperatures up to eighteen hundred degrees Farenheit. It was located in a concrete shed, unmarked and industrial, next to the parking lot of the funeral home. The furnace was warming up. Dad was in it, in a paper box. I opened the furnace. There was no heat yet, but at the back was a circle of flame, ominous in its ferocious, erratic, swirling colors. I looked at this box for a while, then closed the furnace. The director had showed me the jet the initial searing flame would erupt from. It is directly above the chest.

Finally, on the day of the memorial service, I approached

the beleaguered director one final time at the church. Didn't she have the "ashes" (they are not ashes at all, and I prefer the term *relics*) out in her car? She did. Would she please bring them in, quietly, so I could see them. Conspiratorially, with a wink and a squeeze of my forearm, she could. I met her in the back of the hall. She opened the black plastic urn. These relics were remarkable. They looked like a microcosm of a shell-strewn beach—strange and beautiful shapes, chunks of reduced bone, and one startling piece, the size of a quarter, lace-like and delicate. I dipped my fingers in them. Dry and cool. I licked the ash-crusted finger and then rubbed the resulting paste on my forehead in a gesture of intimacy.

The Buddha said that every parent loves their child. In the rapture, love is obscured but my experience is that it is never extinguished. I bow to my father, to my daughter, to my beloved friend Fusho and her father, and to all who are lost in the rapture and to all who are coming home.

Wherever you have been, please join us.

And all shall be well and
All manner of thing shall be well
When the tongues of flame are in-folded
Into the crowned knot of fire
And the fire and the rose are one.
—T. S. Eliot

Afterword

~~~~~~~~~~~~~~~~~~~~~~~~~~~

WHERE DO YOU PUT THE ENERGY NOW?

THE CELESTIAL CHORUSES did not spontaneously burst into song on the day I finished this book. Instead I was depressed. A long labor was over and I didn't know what I had produced. I was certain that my editor would love it. I was just as certain that she would detest it. Here's what else was going on that day.

I was locked in the final day of a battle with a developer who was trying to buy the acreage next to my house. He and his agent were double-dealing with everyone involved and throwing money where I didn't have any to throw. The day before I had done the only thing I knew to do. I called the seller and told him the truth. I wanted that piece of land for my children. I didn't want to drive the deer and coyote and smaller critters away. I didn't have much money, but I'd get a mortgage. So on this day that I finished the book, I was also waiting to hear if the truth mattered against the devil-spawned son-of-a-bitch who wanted to mess with my dream.

In two days I was leaving for Minnesota to lead a week-long workshop putting into practice the theories of the just finished book. How was that going to work?

The next day, I was getting my new teeth. That is not a metaphor. I had had thirteen teeth pulled in fifteen months. Amphetamines and candy bars, now that you ask.

I called my editor to tell her the manuscript was on its way. That was fine with her, but still no sound of heavenly choirs. I told her how nervous I was. She is a wise and sympathetic person and, as she often does, had quite a good suggestion. "Read Natalie's book," she said, referring to *Writing Down The Bones* by Natalie Goldberg. "Which part?" "Any part."

I got the book from the shelf and promptly dropped it. *Goldberg ex machina*, it fell open to the afterword where I read a description of what happened when Natalie finished that book. I related to it entirely, except I hadn't gone out for a glass of wine and two scoops of toffee ice cream. I ate Ben and Jerry's at home. Yes, this is an "alone journey" as Natalie says, and I had felt "the burning through to just pure activity." I saw that "letting go" was the answer or all these problems would own me. So what to do with all that energy?

When my wife came home that night, she was happy that the book was finished, but she had had a rough day at work and needed to chill out. I was on fire and she was going to chill out. None of this was OK and my focus was gone.

At about ten that night I realized I had to take out the garbage. It was snowing and the light from the moon was diffuse at best. I had to haul two large cans a quarter of a mile through the dark and snow, one at a time, to the pick-up point out by the road. That was two trips. A total of a mile of walking. I looked forward to it. I figured that I could get a good adrenaline pump going and then decide what to do with all this energy.

I couldn't hold a thought still. The land. This book. My teeth. The workshop. Where do I put this energy?

Two deer ran across the road directly in front of me about a hundred yards from the main road. The crunch of the snow and the brilliance of brief light reflected from their enormous white tails brought me back. What to do with this energy, this feeling of openness and wonder? Just take out the garbage.

When you're taking out the garbage, just take out the garbage. If we could learn that simple lesson, I think all the rest of it would just take care of itself, don't you?

Happy trails.

Suggested Reading

~~~~~~~~~~~~~~~~~~

Ash, Mel. *The Zen of Recovery*. New York: Jeremy Tarcher/Putnam, 1990.

Bateson, Gregory. *Steps to an Ecology of Mind*. San Francisco: Chandler, 1972.

Dalai Lama, the, and Jean-Claude Carriere. *Violence and Compassion*. New York: Doubleday, 1996.

Epstein, Mark. *Thoughts without a Thinker*. New York: Basic Books, 1995.

Fitzgerald, Kathleen W. *Alcoholism, the Genetic Inheritance*. Lake Forest, Ill.: Whale's Tale Press, 1993.

Franck, Frederick. *A Little Compendium on That Which Matters*. New York: St. Martin's Press, 1993.

Knapp, Caroline. *Drinking, a Love Story*. New York: The Dial Press, 1996.

Loori, John Daido. *The Still Point: A Beginner's Guide to Zen Meditation*. Mt. Tremper, N.Y.: Dharma Communications, 1996.

———. *The Heart of Being*. Mt. Tremper, N.Y.: Dharma Communications, 1996.

Sexson, Lynda. *Ordinarily Sacred*. Charlottesville: University of Virginia, 1992.

Suzuki, Shunryu. *Zen Mind, Beginner's Mind*. New York: Weatherhill, 1970.

Thich Nhat Hanh. *Zen Keys*. New York: Doubleday, 1995.

———. *Peace Is Every Step*. New York: Bantam, 1991.

Trungpa, Chögyam. *The Myth of Freedom*. Boston: Shambhala Publications, 1976.

Vaillant, George E. *The Natural History of Alcoholism*. Cambridge, Mass.: Harvard University Press, 1983.